Y0-ASR-081

HAKIM'S ODYSSEY

FABIEN TOULMÉ

HAKIM'S ODYSSEY

Book 3: From Macedonia to France

graphic mundi

2018—A HIGH SCHOOL IN THE SOUTH OF FRANCE.

HELLO!

HI FABIEN, HOW ARE YOU?

HELLO!
HELLO!!

PLEASE WELCOME FABiEN TOULMÉ, WHO AS YOU KNOW RECENTLY PUBLiSHED THE FiRST TWO BOOKS OF HAKiM'S ODYSSEY.

AND WE GET TO SPEAK WiTH HiM.

i'M SURE YOU'LL ALL LiSTEN TO HiM CAREFULLY.

HELLO.
THANKS FOR HAVING ME AT YOUR SCHOOL.

BEFORE WE GET TO THE SUBJECT OF REFUGEES...
...SINCE I DON'T KNOW IF ALL OF YOU HAVE HAD A CHANCE TO READ HAKIM'S ODYSSEY...

...I'LL GIVE A BRIEF SUMMARY OF THE STORY.

HAKIM IS A YOUNG SYRIAN WHO I STARTED INTERVIEWING IN 2016.
MY GOAL WAS TO CREATE A TESTAMENT OF A REFUGEE'S JOURNEY IN THE FORM OF A GRAPHIC NOVEL, TO UNDERSTAND THE FACTORS THAT MAKE SOMEONE LEAVE THEIR COUNTRY, DESPITE ALL THE RISKS AND CHALLENGES INVOLVED.

I WANTED TO TELL THE STORY OF ONE OF THESE PEOPLE, WHO ARE OFTEN DESCRIBED IN VERY GENERIC TERMS.
MIGRANTS, REFUGEES...

...AND TO SHOW HOW THEIR JOURNEY INTO EXILE IS TRULY AN ODYSSEY.

AND YOU MIGHT'VE HAD TO GO THROUGH IT YOURSELVES IF YOU'D BEEN BORN IN A COUNTRY LIKE SYRIA.

GETTING BACK TO HAKIM, HE DIDN'T START OUT HAVING ANY REASON TO LEAVE SYRIA: HE'D STARTED A NURSERY THAT WAS DOING WELL, HE'D JUST BOUGHT AN APARTMENT, HE WAS SURROUNDED BY HIS FAMILY AND FRIENDS.

HE WAS HAPPY IN HIS COUNTRY.

THEN, IN 2011, PROTESTS BROKE OUT AGAINST THE GOVERNMENT. THE SUBSEQUENT CRACKDOWN WAS BLOODY, AND HAKIM WAS ARRESTED AND TORTURED FOR HELPING WOUNDED PROTESTERS.

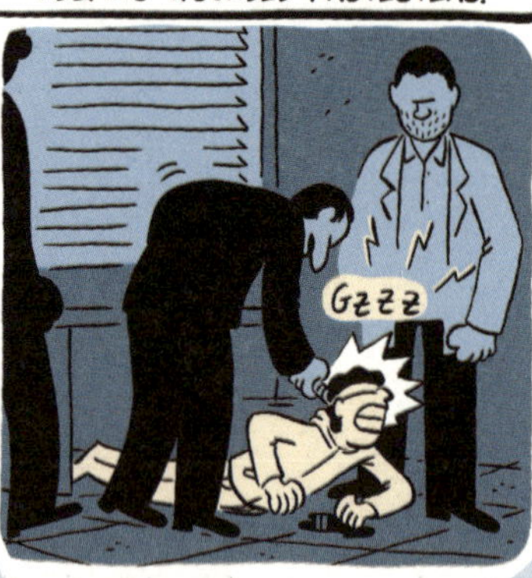

WHEN HE GOT OUT OF PRISON, THE COUNTRY WAS SINKING DEEPER AND DEEPER INTO CIVIL WAR: HIS BUSINESS HAD BEEN SEIZED BY THE ARMY AND HIS APARTMENT WAS DESTROYED IN THE BOMBINGS.

A FEW WEEKS LATER, ONE OF HIS BROTHERS (JAWAD) WAS ARRESTED AT A PROTEST AND IS STILL MISSING TO THIS DAY.

FEARING FOR HIS SAFETY, HAKIM DECIDED TO LEAVE SYRIA, ALONE, UNTIL THINGS CALMED DOWN. HIS PLAN WAS JUST TO GET AWAY FOR A WHILE FROM A PLACE WHERE HIS LIFE WAS AT RISK. HE WASN'T PLANNING TO COME TO EUROPE.

FIRST HE TRIED MOVING TO LEBANON, A COUNTRY NEIGHBORING SYRIA. BUT THERE THEY WERE EXPERIENCING AN INFLUX OF REFUGEES FROM SYRIA, AND IT WAS VERY DIFFICULT FOR HIM TO FIND A JOB SO HE COULD STAY THERE.

SO HE LEFT FOR JORDAN, WHERE HE RAN INTO THE SAME PROBLEMS.

SO HE DECIDED TO GO STAY WITH A FRIEND IN TURKEY, IN THE SOUTHERN CITY OF ANTALYA, WHERE HE HOPED THAT THINGS WOULD BE BETTER.

WHILE HE STILL COULDN'T FIND WORK THERE, HE DID MEET NAJMEH, A YOUNG SYRIAN WOMAN WHO'D BEEN LIVING IN TURKEY WITH HER FAMILY SINCE THE WAR STARTED.

AFTER SEVERAL MONTHS THEY GOT MARRIED, AND IN AN UNEXPECTED TURN OF EVENTS, NAJMEH BECAME PREGNANT. GIVEN THE COUPLE'S PRECARIOUS CIRCUMSTANCES, THIS REALLY COMPLICATED THINGS.

NAJMEH'S PARENTS WERE ALSO STRUGGLING TO FIND WORK, SO THEY ALL DECIDED TO MOVE TO ISTANBUL, A CITY THAT SEEMED TO OFFER MORE OPPORTUNITIES THAN ANTALYA.

IT WAS IN ISTANBUL THAT HADI, NAJMEH AND HAKIM'S SON, WAS BORN.

BUT THIS MOMENT OF JOY WAS BRIEF.

UNFORTUNATELY, CONDITIONS THERE FOR REFUGEES WERE HARDLY BETTER THAN IN ANTALYA, AND NAJMEH'S FATHER, WITH NO OTHER WAY TO KEEP HIS FAMILY ALIVE, DECIDED TO TRAVEL ILLEGALLY (BY PLANE) TO FRANCE, A COUNTRY HE'D VISITED WHEN HE WAS YOUNGER AND WHOSE LANGUAGE HE SPOKE.

WHEN HE ARRIVED, HE WAS GRANTED REFUGEE STATUS AND HE WAS ABLE TO GO THROUGH A FAMILY REUNIFICATION PROCESS, MEANING HIS FAMILY COULD LEGALLY JOIN HIM...

...EXCEPT FOR HAKIM AND HADI, FOR WHOM THE PROCESS WAS MORE COMPLEX.

SO THE TWO OF THEM STAYED IN ISTANBUL FOR MONTHS WHILE THEY WAITED FOR THEIR CASE TO BE RESOLVED, BUT A SERIES OF UNFORTUNATE CIRCUMSTANCES DASHED ANY HOPE OF THEM BEING ABLE TO GET A FRENCH VISA.

SO YOU GOT MARRIED THIS YEAR?
NO, IN 2013.

THEN WHY DOES YOUR MARRIAGE CERTIFICATE SAY 2015?

STUCK IN AN IMPOSSIBLE SITUATION, HAKIM MADE THE CHOICE, DESPITE THE RISKS INVOLVED, TO COME TO FRANCE WITH HIS SON.

THEY WENT TO IZMIR, IN TURKEY, WHERE THEY TOOK OFF IN AN INFLATABLE BOAT FOR THE GREEK ISLAND OF SAMOS.

THEY NEARLY DROWNED DURING THE CROSSING, BUT THEY EVENTUALLY MADE IT.

FROM SAMOS, THEY GOT TO ATHENS, WHERE THEY TOOK A BUS HEADED FOR MACEDONIA.

AND THAT'S WHERE BOOK 2 LEAVES OFF.

THANKS, FABIEN! LET'S GET TO QUESTIONS.

IF YOU HAVE ANYTHING YOU WANT TO ASK, GO AHEAD.

JUST ONE QUICK NOTE...

I DID, OF COURSE, DO MY RESEARCH IN WRITING HAKIM'S ODYSSEY.

BUT I'M NOT A HISTORIAN, OR AN ECONOMIST, OR AN EXPERT ON MIGRANT ISSUES.

SO I'LL TRY TO RESPOND WITH MY WORDS AND MY POINT OF VIEW AS AN AUTHOR, AND BE AS HONEST AS POSSIBLE.

SO, QUESTIONS?

YES?

WHAT EXACTLY IS THE DIFFERENCE BETWEEN A MIGRANT AND A REFUGEE?

WELL, A MIGRANT IS SOMEONE WHO GOES FROM ONE COUNTRY TO ANOTHER, FOR REASONS THAT COULD BE RELATED TO POLITICS, CLIMATE, ECONOMICS, OR SOMETHING ELSE.

THE TERM "REFUGEE" REFLECTS A STATUS DEFINED BY INTERNATIONAL LAW. IT INDICATES SOMEONE WHO'S BEEN GRANTED ASYLUM IN ANOTHER COUNTRY BECAUSE THEY WERE FORCED TO FLEE FROM A MORTAL DANGER IN THEIR OWN COUNTRY.
BOOM!

SO A REFUGEE IS A MIGRANT...

MAY
APR
MAR
FEB
JAN

...BUT A MIGRANT DOESN'T NECESSARILY HAVE REFUGEE STATUS.
YOUR APPLICATION FOR ASYLUM HAS BEEN DENIED...

*SOURCE: FRENCH OFFICE FOR THE PROTECTION OF REFUGEES AND STATELESS PERSONS (OFPRA)

*15 DAYS TO SEVERAL MONTHS ACCORDING TO OFPRA.
**EXCEPT IN THE CASE WHERE REVIEW OF THEIR APPLICATION IS DELAYED BY MORE THAN 9 MONTHS.

*FOR EXAMPLE, €200/MONTH FOR ONE PERSON AND €500/MONTH FOR A FAMILY OF 4 LIKE HAKIM'S

MY DAD SAYS IT'S REALLY EXPENSIVE FOR FRANCE AND THERE'S A RISK THEY'LL TAKE JOBS FROM THE FRENCH. IS THAT TRUE?

IT'S A TOUGH QUESTION. I'M NOT SURE I'M REALLY QUALIFIED TO ANSWER IT.

WHAT WE DO KNOW IS THAT, ON THE ONE HAND, IT COSTS FRANCE A CONSIDERABLE AMOUNT TO TAKE IN ASYLUM SEEKERS, BUT ON THE OTHER HAND, MIGRANTS' PARTICIPATION IN A COUNTRY'S ECONOMY ALSO HAS BENEFITS.
COST
BENEFITS

IN ANY CASE, ECONOMISTS WHO HAVE RESEARCHED THIS ISSUE AGREE THAT THE LONG-TERM, OVERALL BALANCE IS ON THE SIDE OF THE HOSTS BENEFITING.*
COST
BENEFITS
*NOTABLY, IN A STUDY PUBLISHED IN JUNE 2018, RESEARCHERS WORKING FOR THE FRENCH GOVERNMENT INVESTIGATED THE ISSUE OF ASYLUM SEEKERS USING DATA FROM 15 EUROPEAN COUNTRIES AND FOUND THAT AN INFLUX OF MIGRANTS INCREASED PER-CAPITA GDP BY 0.32% OVER 2 YEARS.

IN TERMS OF THESE "JOBS THEY'LL TAKE FROM THE FRENCH," IT'S OFTEN BEEN SHOWN THAT MIGRANTS FILL LABOR SHORTAGES IN PARTICULAR SECTORS THAT ARE NOT REALLY APPEALING TO CITIZENS OF THE HOST COUNTRY (CONSTRUCTION, HUMAN SERVICES...).*
*ACCORDING TO ANTHONY DO (A RESEARCHER AT CEPII, THE CENTER FOR PROSPECTIVE STUDIES AND INTERNATIONAL INFORMATION), "IN THE LONG TERM, STUDIES AGREE THAT IMMIGRATION DOES NOT HAVE A NEGATIVE EFFECT ON EMPLOYMENT."

THERE, I HOPE MY EXPLANATIONS WERE CLEAR ENOUGH.
LET'S HAVE ONE LAST QUESTION?

SO AFTER MACEDONIA, WHAT HAPPENED TO HAKIM?

AH, WELL YOU'LL FIND OUT IN BOOK 3, WHICH I'M WORKING ON NOW.

IN FACT, I HAVE TO GET GOING. I HAVE TO MEET HIM FOR AN INTERVIEW.

IN ANY CASE, THANKS FOR HAVING ME AND FOR ALL YOUR QUESTIONS!

THANK YOU, FABIEN.
YOUR ANSWERS WERE VERY HELPFUL.

GOOD LUCK WITH THE LAST BOOK.

HELLO, HAKIM?

YES, I'M LEAVING NOW. I'LL BE THERE IN AN HOUR.
P

SEE YOU SOON.

Chapter 12: Macedonia and Serbia (September 2015)

"IF WE STAY HERE, WE'LL FREEZE TO DEATH."

I'D NOW BEEN MEETING WITH HAKIM FOR A YEAR AND A HALF TO LISTEN TO HIM TALK ABOUT HIS JOURNEY FROM SYRIA.
WE WERE NEARING THE END OF THIS STORY, WHICH MADE ME BOTH HAPPY AND A LITTLE SAD.

HAKIM!

HI, FABIEN! I DIDN'T EXPECT YOU SO SOON.
YES, SORRY, I'M A LITTLE EARLY. I THOUGHT THERE WOULD BE MORE TRAFFIC.

WHAT ARE YOU DOING?
I WASH THE CHAIRS AT THIS RESTAURANT.
THE OWNER PAYS ME €20 FOR IT.

RIGHT NOW, THINGS ARE A LITTLE TRICKY IN TERMS OF MONEY.
SINCE I HAVEN'T FOUND A STEADY JOB, I'M DOING ODD JOBS WHILE I LOOK FOR SOMETHING BETTER.

WANT ME TO COME BACK IN A BIT?
NO, IT'S FINE. I JUST FINISHED.

WAIT HERE. I'LL ONLY BE A MINUTE.

RIGHT THEN, I GOT THE STRANGEST FEELING.

LIKE I WAS DIRECTLY WITNESSING THE STORY THAT HAKIM HAD BEEN TELLING ME FOR MONTHS.
I'D ALWAYS SEEN HIM IN THE CONTEXT OF OUR INTERVIEWS, BUT HERE I WAS LOOKING AT HIS DAILY LIFE AS A "REFUGEE," THE LIFE HE'D DESCRIBED TO ME.

ALRIGHT.
WE CAN GO.

IT SOUNDS SILLY, BUT WHEN I'D LISTENED TO HIS WORDS, I'D NEVER UNDERSTOOD HIS SITUATION SO ACUTELY.

LET'S TRY NOT TO MAKE TOO MUCH NOISE. NAJMEH'S TAKING A NAP.

TEA?
YES, THANKS.

WELL? HOW'S YOUR LITTLE FAMILY?
GOOD, GOOD.

BUT WE'RE ALL A LITTLE TIRED.
SÉBASTIEN DOESN'T SLEEP THROUGH THE NIGHT YET, AND SINCE WE ALL SLEEP IN ONE ROOM...

WE'VE PUT IN A REQUEST FOR LOW-RENT HOUSING. I'M HOPING WE'LL GET A PLACE SOON.
I HOPE SO TOO.

SO, WHERE DID I LEAVE OFF LAST TIME WE SAW EACH OTHER?
YOU WERE LEAVING ATHENS, HEADING FOR MACEDONIA.
OH YES! THAT'S RIGHT.

THE BUS DROVE NORTH FOR SIX HOURS...

THEN IT STOPPED AT A SERVICE AREA.
KAOIL
KAOIL

EEEE
KAOIL
CAFÉ RESTAURANT
Welcome to Greece
KAOIL
KAOIL

HERE, GET OUT!

WHAT?
BUT WE'RE STILL IN GREECE!
THE BORDER IS STILL AHEAD.

HERE, GET OUT.

WHAT DO WE DO?
WHERE DO WE GO?
THERE.

THANKS FOR THE HELPFUL EXPLANATION.

HOW ARE YOU, HAKIM? DID YOU GET TO REST AT ALL?
Welcome to Greece
KAOIL
KAOIL
CAFÉ RESTAURANT

NOT REALLY, BUT HADI DID.
WHICH WAS LUCKY FOR OUR EARS.

ANYWAY, WOULD YOU MIND IF I CHANGE HIS DIAPER BEFORE WE GO ANYWHERE?
NO, WE COULD ALL USE A MOMENT TO FRESHEN UP.
Welcome to Greece
CAFE RESTAURANT
WC
MINI MARKET

VRRR
FUEL

OH, SHOOT!!

I FORGOT THE PACK OF DIAPERS ON THE BUS...

SORRY, HADi, i GUESS WE'LL HAVE TO DO WiTHOUT.

i'M COUNTiNG ON YOU TO TELL ME WHEN YOU NEED TO USE THE POTTY, OK?

THE OWNER OF THE SERViCE CENTER HAD CLEARLY FiGURED OUT HOW TO MAKE MONEY OFF THE iNFLUX OF MiGRANTS.
50%

AGAiN WiTH THiS BUSiNESS OF DiSTRESS...

SO i BOUGHT A BACKPACK, GOOD SHOES, AND A CHANGE OF CLOTHES FOR HADi AND ME.

THANKS!
HAVE A GOOD DAY!

SO YOU GOT YOURSELF KiTTED OUT TOO?
YES.

HERE'S A COFFEE TO WARM YOU UP BEFORE WE LEAVE.
OH THANKS, HOW KiND!

DO YOU KNOW WHERE WE SHOULD GO NOW?

THAT'S A GREAT QUESTiON.

LET'S SEE HERE...

WE ARE RIGHT...

HERE.
IDOMENI

DO YOU WANT TO CROSS THE BORDER?

UH, YES...

THERE'S A PATH BEHIND THE SERVICE CENTER.
YOU'LL SEE, YOU WON'T BE THE ONLY ONES ON IT.

MACEDONIA IS A LITTLE OVER AN HOUR'S WALK FROM HERE.

INDEED, WE WERE NOT THE ONLY ONES.
MINI
KET
IT WAS A PARADE OF MIGRANTS, NOT REALLY HIDDEN OR DISCREET.

THERE WERE PEOPLE SELLING VARIOUS ITEMS ALONG THE ROAD (CIGARETTES, COOKIES, FRUIT...) AT 3 TIMES THEIR NORMAL PRICE.

WE ALSO ENCOUNTERED REFUGEE AID ASSOCIATIONS, FROM WHOM I WAS ABLE TO GET MORE DIAPERS.

THERE WERE EVEN POLICE!

DON'T WORRY!
WE'RE HERE TO ENSURE YOUR SAFETY UNTIL YOU REACH THE BORDER.

SOMETIMES THIEVES ATTACK AND ROB MIGRANTS.
THEY KNOW YOU CARRY CASH.
POLI

IF YOU WANT, THIS AFTERNOON, THERE'S A BUS THAT CAN TAKE YOU UP TO THE BORDER.
AFTER ALL WE'D BEEN THROUGH TO THIS POINT, IT WAS REALLY SURPRISING TO SEE PEOPLE ORGANIZING TO HELP US.

I GUESS THEY REALLY WANTED TO MAKE SURE WE MADE IT THROUGH THEIR COUNTRY.

I THINK THE STORY OF LITTLE ALAN KURDI WAS STARTING TO DRAW SOME ATTENTION AND THERE WAS A GROWING AWARENESS AMONG THE AUTHORITIES.
OF COURSE, THIS DIDN'T LAST, UNFORTUNATELY...

WELL?

NO, WE'LL KEEP MOVING FORWARD SO WE DON'T LOSE ANY TIME.
ESPECIALLY IF THE BORDER ISN'T FAR.

AS YOU WISH.
IN ANY CASE, BE SURE TO STAY IN GROUPS.

AND MAKE SURE YOU STAY ON THE PATH, ALRIGHT?
IN 2 OR 3 KILOMETERS, YOU'LL SEE TRAIN TRACKS.

FOLLOW THEM NORTH, AND YOU'LL BE IN MACEDONIA.
THANKS!

GOOD LUCK!
POLICE

WE STARTED WALKING AGAIN IN THE MIDDLE OF A PROCESSION OF MIGRANTS.

I THOUGHT THERE WOULD BE A CHECKPOINT, A BORDER POST, BUT NO.
IT SEEMED SO SIMPLE.

WE WERE ABLE TO CROSS INTO MACEDONIA WITHOUT ISSUE.
APPARENTLY, IN THE MONTHS THAT FOLLOWED, THE BORDER CROSSING BECAME MORE DIFFICULT.

FOLLOWING THE TRACKS, WE REACHED A TRAIN STATION.
GEVGELIJA STATION

THERE WERE SEVERAL THOUSAND MIGRANTS WAITING TO TAKE A TRAIN TO SERBIA.

IT WAS CLEAR THE WAIT COULD BE VERY LONG.

AND THE STATION HAD BECOME A CAMP.
WHAT ARE WE SUPPOSED TO DO NOW?
NO IDEA...
UNHCR

WE CAME ACROSS A BIG GATHERING.

APPARENTLY THERE WAS GOING TO BE A DEPARTURE TO HELP WITH THE CONGESTION.
WE'RE GOING TO SPLIT YOU INTO GROUPS.

THERE WILL BE SEVERAL TRAINS, SO NO SHOVING!!

YOU, YOU GO HERE!
YOU, OVER THERE!

ANOTHER GROUP, OVER HERE.
THERE!

NOW, EVERYONE SIT DOWN!
QUIETLY!

THERE MUST HAVE BEEN 6 OR 7 GROUPS OF 100 PEOPLE.

I REALIZED THAT I WAS NO LONGER WITH NIHAD'S FAMILY.
?

I WAS DISAPPOINTED TO LOSE MY TRAVELING COMPANIONS, BUT I WASN'T SAD.
I WAS DIRTY, TIRED, AND HUNGRY. AND ABOVE ALL I WAS THINKING ABOUT MY ULTIMATE GOAL: FRANCE.

AFTER A WHILE, SOMEONE CAME BY TO ASK US FOR MONEY FOR OUR TICKETS AND TO GIVE US OUR PASSES.
THANKS!
HERE!
THANKS!

AND THEN WE WAITED THERE FOR A FEW HOURS, JUST SITTING BY THE TRACKS.
POLICE

FINALLY, A TRAIN ARRIVED AND TWO GROUPS GOT ON IT.
THEN ANOTHER TRAIN AND TWO MORE GROUPS.

THEY CALLED MY GROUP FOR THE THIRD TRAIN.
IT MUST HAVE BEEN 8 P.M.

THE TRAIN WAS OLD AND FILTHY.

IT WAS PACKED AND I DIDN'T HAVE ROOM TO SIT DOWN.
WAAAAH

I STOOD FOR THE WHOLE THREE-HOUR JOURNEY WITH HADI IN MY ARMS.
WAAAH
AFTER EVERYTHING WE'D GONE THROUGH, I WAS EXHAUSTED, AND I STILL HAD A LOT AHEAD OF ME.

THE TRAIN ARRIVED A LITTLE BEFORE MIDNIGHT AT A SMALL STATION IN NORTHERN MACEDONIA.
SERS

THIS WAY!
THIS WAY!

TWO POLICE OFFICERS SHOWED US WHERE TO GO.
THIS WAY!
THIS WAY!

SO WE FOLLOW THE TRACKS?
YES.
HOW FAR?
THERE WILL BE OTHER POLICE OFFICERS ALONG THE WAY.

I WAS ON MY LAST LEGS.

I HAD BLISTERS ON MY FEET FROM MY NEW SHOES.

MY BACK HURT (I'D BEEN CARRYING HADI FOR SEVERAL HOURS).

AND I THOUGHT TO MYSELF THAT I COULDN'T KEEP WALKING FOR LONG.

BUT IT SEEMS THAT DESPAIR GIVES YOU STRENGTH THAT YOU'D NEVER KNOW YOU HAD OTHERWISE.
I KEPT GOING FOR 4 MORE HOURS.

IT WAS AN EXHAUSTING WALK IN THE PITCH DARK.

THE ROAD WAS ROUGH AND YOU COULDN'T STOP, BECAUSE YOU HAD TO MAKE SURE YOU DIDN'T GET LEFT BY YOURSELF.

NO ONE SPOKE, EACH OF US IN OUR OWN THOUGHTS, FIGHTING OUR OWN BATTLE.

AFTER A FEW HOURS OF WALKING, WE NOTICED TENTS DOWN BELOW US.

SOME POLICE SIGNALED TO US.
COME ON DOWN!

POLICIJA
YOU'RE NOW IN SERBIA.

SO WHERE DO WE GO NOW?
YOU HAVE TO BE REGISTERED TO GET A PASS FOR SERBIA.

IN THE NEXT TOWN, THERE'S A REGISTRATION CENTER. YOU HAVE TO GET IT DONE THERE.
YOU'LL NEED IT IN ORDER TO CONTINUE YOUR JOURNEY.

IF YOU WANT, YOU CAN REST HERE, UNDER OUR PROTECTION, AND WAIT UNTIL MORNING.
POLICIJA
THE CENTER OPENS AT 8 A.M.
OTHERWISE, YOU CAN KEEP FOLLOWING THE TRACKS TO THE TOWN.

SOME PEOPLE CHOSE TO STOP FOR A WHILE.
OTHERS PREFERRED TO KEEP GOING, TO GET TO THE REGISTRATION CENTER SOONER.

THAT'S WHAT I PICKED.

I COULDN'T TAKE MUCH MORE, BUT I WANTED THIS PART TO BE OVER.

WE FINALLY GOT TO THE TOWN AROUND 4 OR 5 A.M.

IT WAS FREEZING COLD AND WE WEREN'T DRESSED FOR IT.

LOOK, THAT MUST BE THE REGISTRATION CENTER.

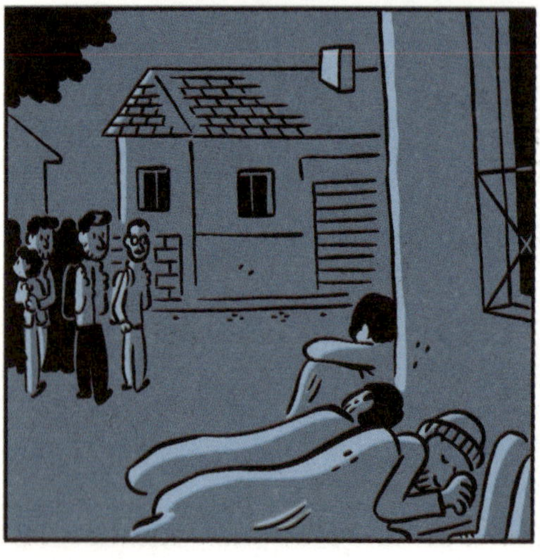

I WAS REALLY WORN OUT.

DADDY'S GOING TO REST A LITTLE, HADI.

TRY TO SLEEP A BIT MORE, SWEETIE.

WE DOZED THERE FOR AN HOUR OR TWO.

BEFORE THE COLD WOKE US UP.
CLACK!
CLACK!
CLACK!

MIIIILK!

LET'S GO. DADDY WILL GET YOU SOME.
ANYWAY, IF WE STAY HERE, WE'LL FREEZE TO DEATH.

I JUST HOPE WE'LL BE ABLE TO FIND WARM WATER AT THIS TIME OF NIGHT.

HELLO.

DO YOU HAVE WARM WATER SO I CAN MAKE HIS BOTTLE?
?

MAYBE I'LL TRY ENGLISH.
BEER 3€
WINE 3€
COFFEE 1€
SODA 2€

"FOR BOTTLE."
"WARM WATER."

OK.
OH, GREAT!
I'LL ALSO HAVE A COFFEE.

IT'S ALMOST READY.
FSHHH!

€2, PLEASE.
WHAT? IT SAYS COFFEE IS €1.

COFFEE €1.
WATER €1.

MIIILK!

IT'S COMING, SWEETIE!

THP! THP!

HEY!!
FOR €500, I'LL TAKE YOU TO BELGRADE!!

C'MON!
NO, THANKS...
AFTER EVERYTHING WE'D BEEN TOLD, I DIDN'T TRUST HIM.

WE'LL COME!
AND HE WAS CHARGING AN ARM AND A LEG.

ANYWAY, I THOUGHT IT SEEMED WISER TO GET REGISTERED.

AT 8 A.M., THE CENTER OPENED.
CLANG!

STAY CALM!
DON'T PUSH!
POLICIJA

FORM A LINE!
ICIJA

THERE WERE TONS OF US.
HEY, I WAS HERE FIRST!
LIKE HELL YOU WERE! I SLEPT AT THE GATE.

AND THE WAIT SEEMED VERY, VERY LONG.

THEY ONLY LET A FEW OF US IN AT A TIME.
STOP!
THAT'S ENOUGH FOR NOW.

AND...

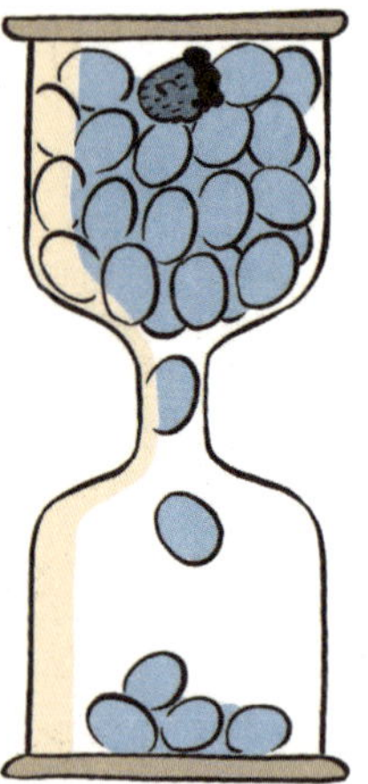

TIME...

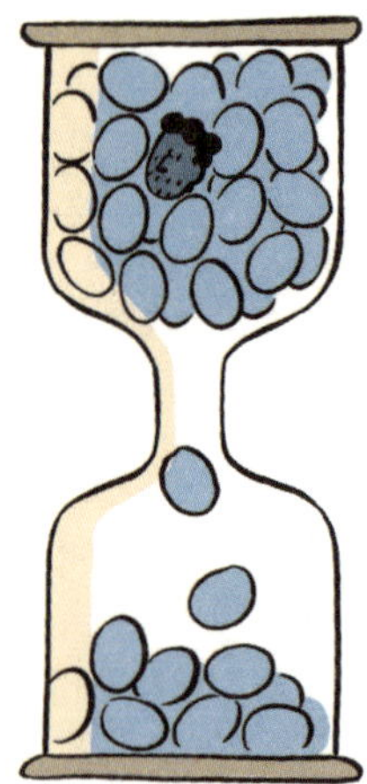

WENT...

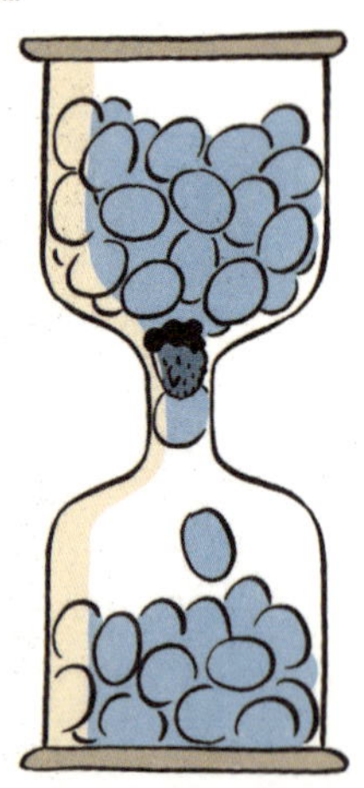

BY...

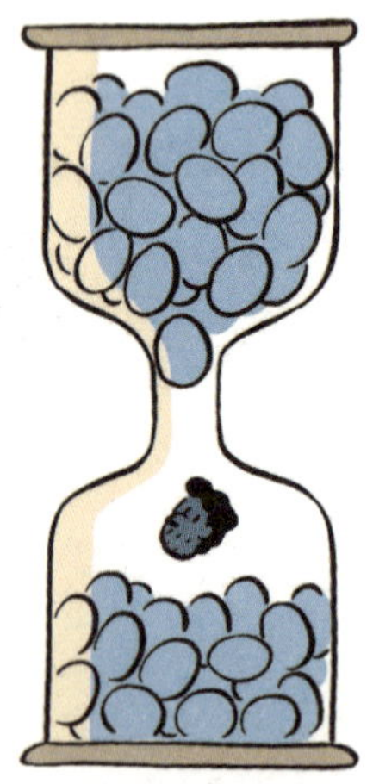

UNTIL FINALLY I WAS GIVEN A PAPER.
HERE YOU GO!
THANKS!

THIS DOCUMENT TRACES YOUR ROUTE.

TO FINALIZE YOUR REGISTRATION, WE'LL TAKE YOUR PHOTO AND GET YOUR FINGERPRINTS.
OK!

BUT YOU'LL HAVE TO COME BACK TOMORROW. THE CENTER IS CLOSING.

IF ANYONE STOPPED ME, I'D FIGURE SOMETHING OUT.

FOLLOWING SOME OTHER REFUGEES, i CAME TO A BUS STATION.

DO YOU KNOW WHERE THIS BUS iS GOiNG?
BELGRADE.

i WAS LUCKY; THAT'S WHERE i NEEDED TO GO.

A LiTTLE REST BEFORE THE NEXT BiT...

CAN i SiT HERE?
YES.

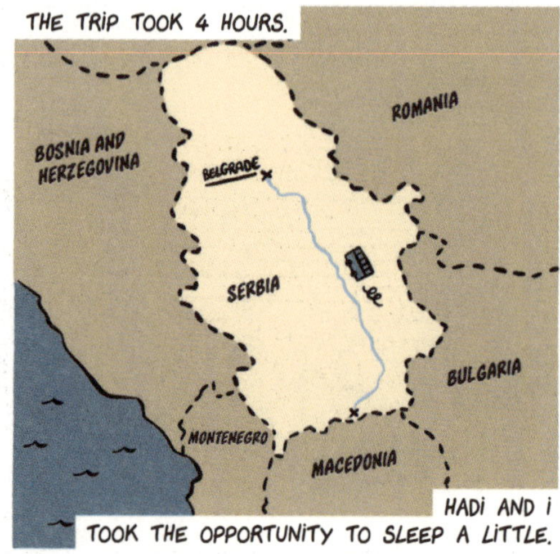
THE TRiP TOOK 4 HOURS.
ROMANIA
BOSNIA AND HERZEGOVINA
BELGRADE
SERBIA
BULGARIA
MONTENEGRO
MACEDONIA
HADi AND i TOOK THE OPPORTUNiTY TO SLEEP A LiTTLE.

THE BUS DROPPED US OFF AROUND 11 P.M. RIGHT IN DOWNTOWN, IN FRONT OF A BIG PARK.
PARK LUKA ĆELOVIĆ

THERE WERE HUNDREDS OF OTHER REFUGEES.

HELLO!
UH...HELLO!
ARE YOU SYRIAN TOO?

Y- YES.
YOUR KID MUST BE HUNGRY. SIT WITH US, WE'LL GIVE YOU SOME SOUP.

THANKS, THAT'S VERY KIND.
OF COURSE.
WE SYRIANS GOTTA HELP EACH OTHER.

HERE, KIDDO!
FANK!

SLUUURP!
FRSH!
FRSH!

WHAT ARE YOU DOING?

WE'RE LOOKING FOR THE BEST WAY TO GET TO AUSTRIA.

WE CAN'T GO THROUGH HUNGARY AT THE MOMENT. IT'S TOO RISKY.
GERMANY
SLOVAKIA
UKRAINE
SWITZERLAND
AUSTRIA
HUNGARY
ITALY
CROATIA
ROMANIA
SERBIA
BULGARIA
MACEDONIA
GREECE

BUT GOING THROUGH CROATIA IS TRICKY: THE WAY IS A LITTLE LONGER AND YOU HAVE TO CROSS THROUGH SLOVENIA TOO.
GERMANY
SLOVAKIA
UKRAINE
SWITZERLAND
AUSTRIA
HUNGARY
SLOVENIA
CROATIA
ROMANIA
BOSNIA AND HERZEGOVINA
SERBIA
BULGARIA
ITALY
ALBANIA
MACEDONIA
GREECE

WHAT'S GOING ON IN HUNGARY?

YOU DIDN'T HEAR WHAT'S BEEN HAPPENING THERE THE PAST FEW WEEKS?
NO.

THE GOVERNMENT'S DOING EVERYTHING IT CAN TO STOP MIGRANTS FROM COMING IN.
AND IF THEY DO, THE POLICE ARREST THEM.
APPARENTLY, THEY'RE PUTTING UP BARBED WIRE ALONG THEIR BORDER.

THE PRESIDENT SAYS WE'RE INVADERS.
THEY TAKE ALL OF US FOR TERRORISTS.
SO THE POLICE ARE REALLY CRACKING DOWN.

A FEW DAYS AGO, THEY USED TEAR GAS AND WATER CANNONS TO DISPERSE SOME MIGRANTS AT THE BORDER.

THEY EVEN BROUGHT IN MILITARY VEHICLES. CAN YOU BELIEVE IT?
THEY ARRESTED MORE THAN 300 PEOPLE AND THE NEWSPAPERS SAY THEY COULD GET 3 YEARS IN PRISON.

PLUS, THANKS TO THE DUBLIN CONVENTION, IF THE HUNGARIAN POLICE ARREST YOU, YOU LOSE EVERYTHING.
WHAT??

ON THE EU LEVEL, THEY HAVE A DATABASE OF ASYLUM APPLICATIONS.
THAT MEANS YOU CAN'T APPLY IN MULTIPLE COUNTRIES.

IN PRACTICE, IT MEANS THAT IF THEY ARREST YOU IN HUNGARY, YOU'RE REGISTERED AS AN ASYLUM SEEKER THERE, AND HUNGARY PROCESSES YOUR APPLICATION.
YOU'RE STUCK WITH THEM.

I HAVE A FRIEND WHO GOT "REGISTERED" IN HUNGARY.
WHEN HE GOT TO THE NETHERLANDS TO FILE HIS APPLICATION THERE, THEY SENT HIM BACK TO HUNGARY.

AND NO ONE WANTS TO LINGER IN HUNGARY.
THEIR REFUGEE CAMPS ARE AWFUL.

HERE, LOOK.

IT'S A VIDEO THAT'S GOING AROUND THE INTERNET RIGHT NOW. IT WAS FILMED BY A VOLUNTEER AT THE CAMP.

THE VIDEO SHOWED A HUNDRED MIGRANTS, INCLUDING CHILDREN, CROWDED BEHIND FENCES IN A HUGE ROOM.

THE POLICE, GROUPED TOGETHER IN FRONT OF THEM AND WEARING MASKS, THREW A FEW SANDWICHES TO THEM.
POLIC

ON EITHER SIDE OF THIS CROWD, YOU COULD SEE OVERCROWDED DORMITORIES.

SO THAT'S WHY WE'RE THINKING OF GOING THROUGH CROATIA INSTEAD.

ESPECIALLY WITH YOUR KID, I'D DEFINITELY SAY YOU SHOULD AVOID HUNGARY.

I'LL HAVE TO THINK ABOUT ALL THIS!

WELL, I'LL TAKE MY LEAVE.
THANKS AGAIN FOR THE SOUP.
NO PROBLEM.

AND GOOD LUCK!
YOU TOO!

I COULDN'T IMAGINE SPENDING THE NIGHT IN THAT COLD WITH HADI, SO I WENT LOOKING FOR A HOTEL.
ADIOTOURS
ΟΠΕΚΑΡΑ
H

BUT IN THAT AREA, THEY WERE ALL TOO EXPENSIVE FOR ME.

I'M EXHAUSTED...

HELLO, MA'AM.
HELLO.
DO YOU KNOW OF ANY AFFORDABLE HOTELS AROUND HERE?

LUCKILY, SHE SPOKE ENGLISH.
IF YOU LIKE, I HAVE A ROOM AT MY PLACE.
YOUR PLACE?

YES, I RENT OUT ROOMS IN MY APARTMENT.
DRVA
I HAVE SEVERAL.
I CHARGE €20.
GREAT, THAT WORKS.

BUT YOU HAVE TO PAY UP FRONT, AND I'LL NEED YOUR PAPERS.
WHAT PAPERS?
THE ONES THEY GAVE YOU WHEN YOU GOT TO SERBIA. YOU SHOULD HAVE TWO.

WHY DO YOU NEED THEM?
SO NO ONE ACCUSES ME OF HARBORING MIGRANTS ILLEGALLY.

HERE, THIS IS MY PAPER.
THE OTHER?

i DIDN'T GET iT...
THE WAiT WAS TOO LONG AND i DIDN'T WANT TO SPEND ANOTHER NiGHT OUTSiDE WiTH MY SON.

GiVE ME THE MONEY. WE'LL MAKE iT WORK.

THANKS.

i'M DOiNG THiS FOR YOUR SON.
SO HE iSN'T SLEEPiNG OUTSiDE iN THE COLD.

THIS WAY!

HERE'S YOUR ROOM.

AND THE WIFI PASSWORD.

THE BATHROOM'S THROUGH HERE.
IF YOU NEED ANYTHING, THERE'S A 24-HOUR CONVENIENCE STORE TWO BLOCKS AWAY.

GOOD NIGHT!
AND PLEASE, NO NOISE, MY ROOM IS RIGHT NEXT DOOR.

I SPENT ALMOST AN HOUR IN THE BATH WITH HADI.

IT WAS SO NICE, I FELT LIKE IT HAD BEEN FOREVER SINCE I'D LAST BATHED.

HADI WENT TO SLEEP AND I CONNECTED TO THE WIFI.
ZZZ

Where are you, Hakim? How are things?
Say hello to your family for me!
Firas
Update us when you
Ahmed
Please, tell us what's going on!
Fahd
I'm in Izmir! You still around?
Osama
Have you made the crossing?
Jihad
May Allah
Zahir
I hope nothing happened

AND AMONG ALL MY MESSAGES:

Najmeh
Answer me, Hakim!! Please!!

I CALLED HER RIGHT AWAY, DESPITE HOW LATE IT WAS.

RiiNG!
RiiNG!

HAKiiiiM!
OH MY GOD!

QUIETER, NAJMEH, YOU'LL WAKE UP HADi AND THE WOMAN SLEEPiNG NEXT TO US.

WOMAN?
WHAT WOMAN SLEEPiNG NEXT TO YOU??

HAHA!
SORRY, i PHRASED THAT WEiRDLY.

i'M RENTiNG A ROOM iN A WOMAN'S HOUSE.
SHE'S SLEEPiNG iN THE NEXT ROOM.

ALLAH IS GREAT! YOU'RE ALIVE!!
HOW ARE YOU, HAKIM?
AND MY BABY?

YOUR BABY'S DOING GREAT, LOOK.

WE'RE IN BELGRADE, IN SERBIA.

WE'VE BEEN THROUGH A LOT BUT WE'RE WELL.
I'LL GIVE YOU THE DETAILS ONCE WE'RE THERE.
WHICH WILL BE SOON, JUST A FEW DAYS, INSH'ALLAH!

AND HOW ARE YOU?
I'M ALRIGHT NOW. I'M SO RELIEVED, SO HAPPY.

I'VE BEEN CRYING NONSTOP FOR THE LAST FEW DAYS.

NOW I'M CRYING AGAIN, SEE?
FROM JOY.

HAHA, I'M SO GLAD TO BE TALKING TO YOU.
IF YOU KNEW...

AFTER NAJMEH, I CALLED MY FAMILY IN SYRIA.
I TALKED TO EVERYONE: MY BROTHERS AND SISTERS, MY MOTHER.
SHE CRIED A LOT... AS DID I.

THEN WHEN I HUNG UP, GLANCING THROUGH MY MESSAGES:
NIHAD
Hi Hakim. We're in Belgrade, How about you?
HE'D SENT IT THAT SAME DAY.

I ANSWERED RIGHT AWAY.
I'm in Belgrade too. I just found a place to sleep.
TAP!
TAP!

BZZZ
Haha, amazing!! We're looking for a place to stay, do you know where we can find a hotel room?

TAP!
TAP!
Wait just a sec.

KNOCK!
KNOCK!

KNOCK!
KNOCK!
KNOCK!
KNOCK!

WHAT?!
WHAT DO YOU WANT?

EXCUSE ME, MA'AM. I HAVE A FRIEND WHO'S LOOKING FOR A PLACE TO SLEEP.
DO YOU HAVE ANY ROOMS FREE?

...

YES...
TELL HIM HE CAN COME.

HELLO.
HELLO, COME IN!

OH! THERE'S FOUR OF YOU?

I ONLY HAVE ONE OPEN ROOM AND EVEN WITH THREE IT'LL BE VERY TIGHT.
IT'S USUALLY FOR ONE PERSON.

IF YOU WANT, NIHAD, ONE OF YOUR SONS CAN STAY WITH ME.
YOU'RE SURE?
IT WOULDN'T BOTHER YOU?

NO, NOT AT ALL.

NIHAD GAVE THE WOMAN EVERYTHING SHE NEEDED (BOTH DOCUMENTS, THE MONEY) AND WE WENT TO BED.
GOODNIGHT!
'NIGHT!
IT WAS ALREADY ABOUT THREE IN THE MORNING.

HADi WOKE UP AT 10 A.M., HE WAS HUNGRY.
mmm

i MADE HiM A BOTTLE AND NiHAD'S FAMiLY CAME AND JOiNED US.
DiD YOU SLEEP WELL?
YES, THANKS.
THP THP THP

WE WERE ALL GROGGY WiTH FATiGUE.
i'M GOiNG TO TRY TO FiND SOMETHiNG TO EAT, WANT TO COME?

CAN i LEAVE HADi HERE?
YES, OF COURSE.
NO PROBLEM.

iT WAS SUNDAY. NOTHiNG WAS OPEN.
EKRAN
SAMSUN
THE WOMAN SAiD THERE'S A CONVENiENCE STORE NEARBY.

BiNGO! iT'S OPEN!

WE BOUGHT BREAD, LAUGHING COW CHEESE, AND... CIGARETTES.
I SEE YOU STILL HAVE THAT FILTHY HABIT!

NIHAD TOLD ME HOW THEY'D GOTTEN TO BELGRADE.
KREV KOST
IT WAS MORE OR LESS THE SAME WAY I DID.

AND I SHARED WITH HIM WHAT I'D BEEN TOLD ABOUT HUNGARY.
I'M REALLY NOT SURE.
ESPECIALLY WITH HADI.

I GET IT.
BUT IT CAN'T BE WORSE THAN WHAT WE'VE ALREADY BEEN THROUGH.
I'M SURE YOU'RE RIGHT.

IT WAS ALMOST NOON, AND IF WE DIDN'T WANT TO PAY FOR AN ADDITIONAL NIGHT, WE HAD TO LEAVE SOON.
SEE YOU SHORTLY.
YES.
WE'LL GET READY.

I USED MY LAST MOMENTS OF WIFI TO ASK FOR ADVICE ABOUT HUNGARY FROM MY FRIENDS AND FAMILY.
TAP!
SOME OF THEM TOLD ME TO TRY IT, BUT MOST ADVISED AGAINST GOING THERE.

WELL?
YOU READY?

I HEARD ABOUT A BUS THAT'S ABOUT TO LEAVE FOR THE HUNGARIAN BORDER.
THE SEATS AREN'T TOO EXPENSIVE AND THERE ARE A FEW LEFT.

I THINK I'LL STAY FOR A BIT AND TRY TO FIND A SAFER ALTERNATIVE.
WITH HADI, I'M NOT SURE ABOUT TRYING IT.

OK...
MAYBE WE'LL MEET AGAIN SOMEWHERE ELSE.
IN AUSTRIA OR GERMANY.

WHO KNOWS...

GOODBYE, BROTHER.
AND GOOD LUCK!
YES, YOU TOO.

i PAiD FOR ANOTHER NiGHT iN OUR ROOM AND WENT OUTSiDE TO GET HADi SOME FRESH AiR.
WAAAAAH!
HE GOT UPSET AND STARTED CRYiNG.

CALM DOWN, SWEETiE.

THERE, LOOK, i SEE SOMETHiNG OVER THERE YOU MiGHT LiKE.
?

*WHAT'S YOUR NAME?

*SLIDE, WAIT FOR ME!

IN THE LATE AFTERNOON, WE WENT BACK TO OUR ROOM.
TAP!
TAP!
TAP!
I TALKED WITH FRIENDS ON WHATSAPP FOR A LONG WHILE.

I STILL COULDN'T DECIDE WHERE TO GO NEXT ON MY JOURNEY.
TAP!
TAP!
TAP!
TAP!
I WAS EXTREMELY AFRAID TO GO THROUGH HUNGARY, BUT I DIDN'T HAVE THE FUNDS TO TAKE THE LONGER TRIP THROUGH CROATIA.

WHAT TO DO?
Go through Croatia instead. You'll make do!!
The police can't be everywhere in Hungary.
At worst, they'll let you go quickly if you get taken in.
Don't take the chance, go by the safer road.

BY THE TIME I WENT TO BED, I STILL HADN'T DECIDED.
?!

AND IN THE MORNING I WAS STILL UNSURE.

I WENT BACK TO THE PARK FROM THE FIRST NIGHT TO SEE IF I COULD GET ANY "FRESH" INFORMATION ON HUNGARY.

HUNGARY?
WE'RE GOING TO GO THAT WAY.

I HAVE A FRIEND WHO WENT THERE 3 DAYS AGO AND HE HASN'T RUN INTO ANY REAL TROUBLE YET.

OK.
THANKS...
NO PROBLEM.

IT WAS ALREADY 11:30. I HAD TO MAKE A DECISION.

I COULDN'T STAY HERE FOREVER. IT WAS A NEEDLESS WASTE OF MONEY.

RIING! RIING!
HELLO?

HI, NAJMEH, I'M CALLING TO TELL YOU I'M LEAVING NOW AND WE MIGHT NOT BE ABLE TO TALK AGAIN FOR A BIT.

ALRIGHT, HAKIM.
SO WHAT HAVE YOU DECIDED TO DO?

I'M GOING TO HUNGARY.
BUDAPEST.

GOOD LUCK, MY LOVE.
I'M WITH YOU.
AND WHATEVER HAPPENS, HAPPENS.

LET'S GO, HADI.
WE'RE OFF.

I WENT BACK TO THE PARK, LOOKING FOR A SMUGGLER.

HELLO, I'M TRYING TO GET TO HUNGARY.

IT'S €800.
!
THAT'S WAY TOO MUCH.

BUT NOTHING WILL HAPPEN TO YOU WITH US.
NO RISK OF THE POLICE CATCHING YOU.

SORRY, I CAN'T AFFORD IT.
WAIT!

€500?
TOO MUCH.

I ASKED 3 OR 4 SMUGGLERS THE SAME THING. THE PRICES WERE OUTRAGEOUS, SO I WENT TO FIND A CAB DRIVER.
HELLO, HOW MUCH TO GO TO HUNGARY?

THAT'LL BE €200.

BUT SO YOU'RE AWARE, I'LL DROP YOU 2 KILOMETERS BEFORE THE BORDER INTO HUNGARY.
?

WAIT, YOU CAN MAKE THE SAME TRIP ON A BUS FOR JUST €50.

YEAH BUT IT TAKES FOREVER AND IT'S RISKIER.
THE POLICE OFTEN CHECK THE BUSES.

WHAT DO YOU THINK?

GO WITH GOD, BROTHER!

THE DRIVER STUCK TO BACK ROADS.

DOUBTLESS TO AVOID THE CHECKPOINTS.

AT THE TIME, I DIDN'T NOTICE THIS TYPE OF THING...

...BUT NOW, LOOKING BACK ON IT, ALL THE LANDSCAPES WERE VERY PRETTY AND VERY GREEN. THE FOREST, THE RIVERS...

AFTER 2 HOURS OF DRIVING, THE TAXI STOPPED IN A DESERTED VILLAGE.
ALRIGHT, WE'RE HERE.

FOLLOW THE ROAD, THEN AS YOU'RE LEAVING TOWN, YOU'LL SEE A TRAIL GOING THROUGH THE TREES.

KEEP WALKING FOR ANOTHER 2 KILOMETERS AND YOU'LL GET TO A RAILROAD CROSSING.

THAT'S THE BORDER.

HERE.
THANKS!
GOOD LUCK!

VRRRR

THE VILLAGE WAS SILENT.

THERE WAS NO ONE ON THE STREETS.

↑Kелебија

SO...
AM I IN HUNGARY NOW?

HEY!
PSSSS!

A LITTLE WAYS AWAY, A DOZEN MIGRANTS WERE SITTING IN AN ORCHARD.
HERE!

WHAT ARE YOU DOING?
SIT DOWN AND DON'T MAKE MUCH NOISE!

WE'RE WAITING FOR NIGHT TO CROSS INTO HUNGARY.
OH? I THOUGHT I WAS ALREADY THERE.

NO, NOT QUITE YET.

SEE THAT ROAD?
THAT'S HUNGARY.

BUT THE POLICE DRIVE BY CONSTANTLY.
SO WE'RE WAITING FOR NIGHT.

ALONG THAT ROAD, A LITTLE FARTHER UP, THERE'S A SERVICE STATION WHERE THERE ARE SMUGGLERS WHO CAN TAKE US NORTH.
THAT'S THE PLACE TO GO.

YOU MIGHT BE WONDERING HOW MIGRANTS KNOW ABOUT ALL THIS: THE ROUTES, THE MEETING POINTS WITH THE SMUGGLERS...
IS IT A LONG WALK?

IT'S ACTUALLY THANKS TO CELL PHONES THAT YOU CAN GATHER SO MUCH INFO FROM PEOPLE WHO HAVE GONE THE SAME WAY BEFORE YOU (FROM FACEBOOK, WHATSAPP...).
IT SHOULD BE JUST UNDER TEN KILOMETERS.

OR, LIKE I WAS DOING THEN, YOU CAN RELY ON PEOPLE TO TELL YOU THE WAY TO GO.
VRRR
VRRRR
IT'S NOT SO FAR...
BUT IT'S FAR ENOUGH THAT YOU CAN BE CAUGHT.

AFTER A WHILE, A POLICE CAR STOPPED ON THE SIDE OF THE ROAD.
VRR

CLACK!
CLACK!

COME ON!
DON'T BE AFRAID!

WE GOT BUSES FOR YOU!!

DON'T MOVE. IT'S A TRAP TO TAKE US IN.
WE'RE STILL IN SERBIA. THEY CAN'T COME OVER HERE AND CAPTURE US.

YOU SURE YOU DON'T WANNA COME?

TOO BAD!
IT WON'T CHANGE ANYTHING, ANYWAY. WE'LL CATCH YOU IN THE END!
HAHA!

VRRR

WHAT A BUNCH OF BASTARDS!

NIGHT FELL AND WE SET OFF IN SILENCE, KEEPING A GOOD DISTANCE FROM THE ROAD.
WE WALKED UNDER THE COVER OF THE TREES FOR ABOUT AN HOUR.

THERE, THAT'S THE SERVICE STATION.
WHEN WE GET THERE, WE HAVE TO SPLIT UP SO WE DON'T DRAW ATTENTION.

?

WE DID SPLIT UP, BUT WE CLEARLY DIDN'T LOOK LIKE HUNGARIANS, OR TOURISTS.

I BOUGHT COOKIES AND SOME TEA.

AND I WENT TO SIT IN A CORNER TO CONSIDER WHAT MY NEXT STEP SHOULD BE.

THE ATMOSPHERE WAS REALLY WEIRD.

THE SHOP WAS FULL OF PEOPLE BUT IT WAS VERY QUIET.

PEOPLE FROM MY GROUP WALKED AROUND WITHOUT MAKING EYE CONTACT.

THE HUNGARIANS WATCHED US, SUSPICIOUS.

CHIPS

THERE WAS A SENSE OF FEAR.
A FEELING THAT WE WERE REALLY NOT WELCOME.

CAN I SIT DOWN?

YES, IF YOU LIKE.
HE WAS A SYRIAN KURD, BUT HE DIDN'T REALLY LOOK LIKE A REFUGEE IN TRANSIT.

WANNA GET OUT OF HUNGARY?

UH... YES...

I HAVE A CAR. I CAN GET YOU TO AUSTRIA.
€1000.

NO THANKS.
THAT'S TOO MUCH FOR ME.

ME TOO!
I WANT TO GO.

AFTER A LONG NEGOTIATION, WE MANAGED TO AGREE TO €800 TOTAL (€400 FOR THE OTHER MIGRANT AND €400 FOR ME).

YOU GOTTA GIVE ME THE MONEY NOW.

WHAT?
NO, WE'LL GIVE YOU THE MONEY WHEN WE GET THERE.

NO. I'M TAKING ON A LOT OF RISK.
GIVE IT NOW OR WE'RE DONE HERE.
WE ENDED UP AGREEING. WE DIDN'T HAVE MUCH CHOICE.

WE LEFT THE SHOP FOLLOWING 50 METERS BEHIND HIM, WHICH HE'D ASKED US TO DO TO TRY TO KEEP A LOW PROFILE.

WE MET UP AGAIN AT HIS CAR.

WE DIDN'T SAY A WORD. WE WERE VERY TENSE.
VRRR

WE DROVE FOR ABOUT FIFTY KILOMETERS.

THEN WE CAME TO A TOWN...

HELLO.

HELLO.
WE'RE ALL FRIENDS...

H...
KÉSZENLÉTI
RENDŐRSÉG
HELLO.

THEY LOOKED REALLY THREATENING AND TOUGH.
LIKE THE RUSSIAN VILLAINS IN SOME JAMES BOND MOVIE, HAHA!

GET OUT!

AFTER CHECKING OUR PAPERS, ONE OFFICER SAID:
YOU, THE DRIVER, YOU STAY HERE WITH MY COLLEAGUE.

AND YOU, THE "FRIENDS," YOU COME WITH ME.

GET IN!

THE BUS WAS FILLED WITH MIGRANTS.

AND IT TOOK OFF AS SOON AS WE'D SAT DOWN.
VRRR

THEY TOOK THE DRIVER AND DROVE OFF.

IF WE'D COME THROUGH 5 MINUTES LATER, I'M SURE WE WOULDN'T HAVE RUN INTO THEM.

IT WAS MAKTUB...

Chapter 13: Hungary (September 2015)

"IT'S WHAT I CALL 'HUNGARIAN HOSPITALITY.'"

THE BUS DROVE FOR ABOUT 15 MINUTES.
THEN STOPPED, SEEMINGLY AT RANDOM.

GET OUT!
DON'T TALK!

WE WEREN'T REALLY IN THE MIDDLE OF NOWHERE.

THIS WAY!
IT WAS THE ENTRANCE TO A CAMP.

ALL SURROUNDED BY FENCING.

STOP HERE!

A GUY IN CIVILIAN DRESS—MAYBE FROM THE UN, I'M NOT SURE—STARTED TALKING TO US.
LISTEN TO ME!

HE SPOKE ARABIC.
YOU HAVE TO SHOW US YOUR IDENTITY DOCUMENTS.

WE'LL GET YOU REGISTERED, THEN MY COLLEAGUE WILL GIVE YOU A WRISTBAND.

ON IT WILL BE YOUR IDENTIFICATION NUMBER.

UNDER NO CIRCUMSTANCES SHOULD YOU REMOVE IT. IT'LL BE VERY IMPORTANT LATER.

OK, LET'S BEGIN.
YOUR NAME...
SARDAR AYATOLLAHI.

BY ABOUT MIDNIGHT WE WERE ALL REGISTERED.
GREAT!
NOW YOU CAN GO AND REST.

YOU'LL NEED TO DIVIDE UP AND GO INTO THE TENTS.
YOU CAN TAKE ANY BED THAT'S CURRENTLY OPEN.

NNNN!

LEAVE IT ON, HADI.
THE MAN SAID IT WAS IMPORTANT.

I STILL REMEMBER OUR NUMBERS.
645

AND I FOUND MYSELF WONDERING WHAT THEY WERE FOR...
THEY MADE ME THINK OF INMATE NUMBERS.

EVERY TENT HELD MAYBE TEN BEDS.
ZZZ
ZZZZ
ZZZZ
THEY WERE CANVAS COTS.

ZZZ
NNNN
STOP, HADI!
LEAVE IT ALONE!
ZZZ

GOOD NIGHT, SWEETIE.

I WAS EXHAUSTED, BUT I COULDN'T GET TO SLEEP.
I HAD TOO MANY QUESTIONS.

HOW LONG WERE THEY GOING TO KEEP US HERE?
WOULD THEY TAKE HADI AWAY?
WHAT STATE WOULD NAJMEH BE IN IF I COULDN'T GET WORD TO HER FOR A LONG TIME?
COULD WE STILL GET TO FRANCE?
OR WERE WE REALLY GOING TO HAVE TO SEEK ASYLUM IN HUNGARY?
WHAT WOULD'VE HAPPENED IF I'D CHOSEN CROATIA INSTEAD?
OR IF I'D LEFT WITH NIHAD AND HIS FAMILY?

BLAH BLAH
BLAH BLAH
BLAH BLAH!

IN THE MORNING, WE AWOKE VERY EARLY TO THE SOUND OF THE TENT'S OTHER OCCUPANTS TALKING TO EACH OTHER.

IT WAS 6 A.M. AND WE WERE VERY COLD.

DADDY, MIIILK!

OK, LET'S GO FIND SOME WARM WATER.
DADDY WILL MAKE A BOTTLE.

THROUGH THE FOG, i SAW ABOUT FIFTY PEOPLE WHO SEEMED TO BE WAITiNG FOR SOMETHiNG.
?

PLOTCH!
PLOTCH!

WHAT ARE YOU DOiNG?

WAiTiNG FOR THE OUTHOUSE.

THERE WERE ONLY FOUR TOiLETS TOTAL FOR THE ENTiRE CAMP.
BEHiND THESE OUTHOUSES, THERE WERE FOUR SiNKS FOR WASHiNG UP.

THIS IS THE LINE
FOR THE TOILETS.

FOR THE SINKS,
THE LINE'S ON THE
OTHER SIDE.

WOW!
I HOPE YOU'LL BE
ABLE TO WAIT, HADI.
mmm

EXCUSE ME, IS
THERE WARM
WATER HERE?
IT'S
FOR HIS
BOTTLE.
DADDY
MIIILK
NO, BROTHER,
THERE'S ONLY COLD.

OK, THANKS.
MIIIILK

WAIT!
IF YOU'RE
JUST FILLING HIS
BOTTLE, GO AHEAD!

MIIIILK!
MIIIILK!
YES, COMING!

YIKES!
WE'RE ALMOST OUT OF FORMULA.

HERE, MY HUNGRY BOY.

THP
THP
WAAAAH!

YES, SORRY HADI, IT'S COLD.
BUT THERE'S NO OTHER OPTION.

THERE YOU GO.

AND I WAS STARTING TO FEEL DIZZY.

PFF!
PFF!

HELLO.
HI!

DO YOU KNOW IF THEY'RE GOING TO SERVE US BREAKFAST?
OOF!

YES, THEY DO BREAKFAST.
AND IT SHOULD BE HERE SOON.

BUT DON'T EXPECT TO EAT YOUR FILL.
WE'RE ALL STARVING HERE.

THEY PASS OUT THE SAME FOOD THREE TIMES A DAY.
LITTLE BOLOGNA SANDWICHES.
EVEN FOR THE MUSLIMS?

THE SAME FOR EVERYONE.
IT'S WHAT I CALL "HUNGARIAN HOSPITALITY."

THEY DON'T CARE IN THE LEAST THAT MUSLIMS DON'T EAT PORK.

ANYWAY, I HOPE YOU'RE GOOD AT BASKETBALL!
BASKETBALL?

"NO" PUSHING!
HEY, IT'S STARTING.

C'MON!
STAY CALM!
STAY CALM!

YOU'RE A BASKETBALL STAR!

DADDY!!
YES, DADDY'S HERE!

WAS HE A GOOD BOY?
YES!
VERY GOOD!

'WICH!
YES, IT'S A SANDWICH.
WANT SOME?

YEH!

WE HAVE TO TAKE OFF THE PLASTIC FIRST.

WE ATE THE SANDWICH...
CRUNCH!
CHOMP! CHOMP!
AND I WAS STILL HUNGRY.

NUMBERS 250 TO 260!!

WHAT'S HAPPENING?

EVERY DAY THEY CALL UP 50 PEOPLE AND REGISTER THEIR ASYLUM APPLICATIONS.
THEY TAKE YOUR PRINTS AND PHOTOGRAPH, AND GIVE YOU A TRAIN TICKET TO ANOTHER CAMP.

I HAVE A FRIEND WHO GOT REGISTERED IN HUNGARY.
WHEN HE GOT TO THE NETHERLANDS TO MAKE HIS APPLICATION THERE, THEY SENT HIM BACK TO HUNGARY.

WHAT IF I DON'T WANT TO APPLY FOR ASYLUM HERE?
WELL, THEN YOU STAY HERE.

THERE HAVE BEEN PEOPLE WHO DIDN'T WANT TO...
THEY ALL BROKE AFTER A FEW WEEKS.
LIVING HERE IS TOO HARD.

ARE YOU GOING TO REGISTER?
SOON, INSH'ALLAH!

I'M SICK AND TIRED OF WAITING.
I'VE BEEN HERE FOR 5 DAYS.

NUMBERS 260 TO 270!!

50 PEOPLE PER DAY...

THAT MEANT THAT I STILL HAD AT LEAST 7 DAYS AHEAD OF ME THERE.

MINIMUM.
NUMBERS 270 TO 280!!
AND THAT WAS ONLY IF I AGREED TO BE REGISTERED.

IT WAS A HARD THING TO PROCESS, BUT I TOLD MYSELF AT LEAST I'D HAVE TIME TO THINK.
COME ON.

FOR THE MOMENT, THERE WERE MORE PRESSING NEEDS TO TAKE CARE OF.

EXCUSE ME, DO YOU KNOW WHERE I CAN FIND SOME MILK FOR MY SON?
NO, SORRY!

NO, SORRY!

I FINALLY TRIED BEGGING AN OFFICER.
!

WHAT, YOU THINK THIS IS A HOTEL?
YOU SHOULDA STAYED IN YOUR COUNTRY!!

I DIDN'T FIND ANY MILK, AND FOR 3 DAYS...

HADI HAD TO EAT BOLOGNA SANDWICHES...

AND HE ENDED UP GETTING SICK.

WHICH WAS TRICKY, SINCE I DIDN'T HAVE ANY DIAPERS LEFT.
IS THAT BETTER?
WAAAAH!
SHHHH, SWEETIE.

AND THERE WAS ALWAYS A LINE FOR THE BATHROOMS.
IT WILL PASS.
WAAAAH

THERE WAS NO WAY TO WASH HIM EITHER.

WAAAH!
ONE SECOND, HADI.

SHHH

SO I IMPROVISED USING A CLOTH DAMPENED WITH ICE-COLD WATER.
WAAAAH!
YOU'RE OK, KIDDO.

I FINALLY TOOK HADI TO SEE THE CAMP DOCTOR.

JUST LIKE EVERYWHERE ELSE, THERE WAS A LINE.

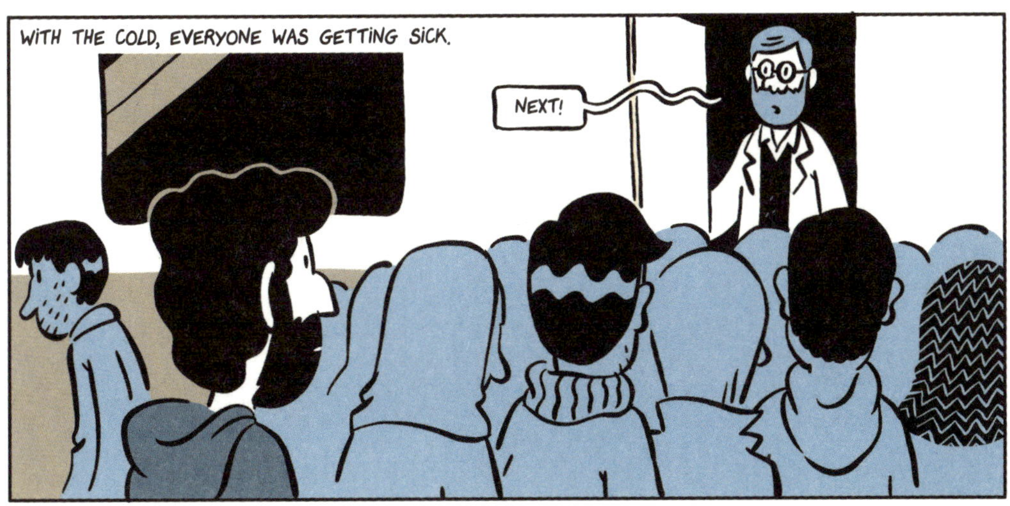
WITH THE COLD, EVERYONE WAS GETTING SICK.
NEXT!

IN FRONT OF ME, THERE WAS A YOUNG BOY WITH A FEVER. HIS MOTHER WAS IN TEARS.

YOU OK?
I CAN'T TAKE IT ANYMORE, I'VE BEEN HERE 15 DAYS, AND I DON'T WANT TO GET REGISTERED.
I WANT TO JOIN MY HUSBAND IN DENMARK.

I TRIED TO COMFORT HER, BUT I FELT AS HELPLESS AS SHE DID.
IT'S ALRIGHT, IT'LL WORK OUT, MA'AM.

THERE WAS ALSO A YOUNG SYRIAN, MAYBE 20 YEARS OLD.
THESE ARE MY NEPHEWS.

THEIR PARENTS ARE DEAD AND I'M BRINGING THEM WITH ME TO GERMANY.

THE YOUNGER ONE HAS STOMACH CRAMPS.

IN THIS CAMP, AND ALL THROUGHOUT MY JOURNEY, I MET SO MANY PEOPLE WHO'D BEEN THROUGH TERRIBLE THINGS IN LIFE.
NEXT!
IF I WROTE BOOKS LIKE YOU, I COULD TELL 200 DIFFERENT STORIES, EACH ONE UNIQUE BUT AT THE SAME TIME SO SIMILAR IN TERMS OF THE DISTRESS, MISFORTUNE, AND MISERY THEY INCLUDE.

AFTER 2 HOURS IN LINE, THE DOCTOR BROUGHT US IN.

HE GAVE ME MILK, DIAPERS, AND MEDICINE FOR HADI.

HE STARTED IMPROVING...
EVEN AS I WAS FEELING WORSE.

REMEMBER, WE DIDN'T HAVE ENOUGH OF ANYTHING, ESPECIALLY FOOD.
GRRRGL!
GRRRGL!
GRRRGL!
GRR

ALSO, THE POPULATION IN THE CAMP JUST KEPT INCREASING.

EVERY DAY, ABOUT 100-150 PEOPLE SHOWED UP.
WHILE ONLY 50 OF US LEFT.

SO OUR LIVING CONDITIONS GOT WORSE AND WORSE.
ANY OPEN BEDS HERE?
ZZZ

NO...
ZZZ

NONE OF THE TENTS HAVE ANY ROOM.
CAN WE SLEEP ON THE FLOOR HERE UNTIL MORNING?

YES, OF COURSE.
COME ON IN!
ZZZZ

THE DAYS WENT BY AND THE OCCUPANTS' DISCONTENTMENT GREW.

AND ABOUT 7 DAYS AFTER MY ARRIVAL...
WE'RE HUNGRY!
?

WE'RE FED UP!

LET US GO!

GET BACK!

CALM IT DOWN!

NUMBERS 550-700, GO GET YOUR STUFF.
YOU'RE LEAVING THE CAMP!
RENDÖRSEG
POLICE

?

NO! WE'RE NOT GOING WITH YOU!!
WE NEED REAL ANSWERS!!

WE'LL GIVE YOU PAPERS TO LEAVE HUNGARY!
BUT FIRST WE HAVE TO TRANSFER YOU TO ANOTHER CAMP!

WHAT?
NO! WE WANT TO LEAVE!
WE DON'T WANT TO REQUEST ASYLUM!
RENDÖRSEG
POLICE

THE PAPERS WE'RE GIVING YOU ARE NOT ASYLUM APPLICATIONS.
THEY'RE JUST PASSES SO YOU CAN LEAVE HUNGARY LEGALLY.

WELL WHY CAN'T WE GET THE PAPERS HERE?
YES, HE'S RIGHT!!

THERE'S TOO MANY OF YOU!
WE DON'T HAVE ENOUGH STAFF TO HANDLE EVERYTHING HERE!
WE HAVE TO TRANSFER YOU.

OK...

EVERYONE FINALLY CALMED DOWN, AND WE WENT TO GRAB OUR THINGS.

WHEN I GOT BACK, THERE WERE THREE BUSES WAITING AT THE GATES.

IT WAS 10 A.M.

ON THE ONE HAND, I FELT FREE.
WE GET TO TAKE OFF OUR WRISTBANDS, HADI.

ON THE OTHER, THE WHOLE THING SEEMED STRANGE TO ME, AND I WONDERED IF IT WAS A TRAP.
NO!
KEEP!

NO, HADI, COME ON!
WE'RE NOT KEEPING THEM...

AFTER A FEW MINUTES OF DRIVING, THE BUSES PARKED AT THE TRAIN STATION IN A NEARBY TOWN.

WE CROWDED INSIDE THE STATION.
LISTEN UP!

WE'RE PUTTING YOU ON A TRAIN TO ANOTHER CAMP SO YOU CAN GET THE PAPERS WE TOLD YOU ABOUT.

THAT TRAIN IS LEAVING IN ONE HOUR.

WHILE WE WAIT, YOU ARE NOT ALLOWED TO LEAVE THE STATION.

ANYWAY, IF YOU DO LEAVE, YOU WON'T HAVE PAPERS AND NO ONE WILL AGREE TO TRANSPORT YOU.
YOU'LL JUST END UP GETTING ARRESTED AND TAKEN BACK TO THE CAMP YOU CAME FROM.

SO NO FUNNY BUSINESS!
GOT IT?

OK!
FINE.

GOOD...

THERE WERE MILITARY PERSONNEL POSTED AT EVERY EXIT, TO MAKE SURE WE DIDN'T GET AWAY.

OK, HADI, DADDY'S GOING TO MAKE A QUICK BATHROOM STOP.

HEY, KIDDO.
PLIC!
PLIC!
PLIC!
FSHH

FSHH

HEY YOU!
WANNA LEAVE?

W- WHAT?
THERE AREN'T ANY OFFICERS AT THE CLOSEST ENTRANCE.
IF YOU WANNA GO, NOW'S THE TIME.

IN MY MIND, IT ALL HAPPENED SO FAST.
IT MIGHT HAVE BEEN RECKLESS BUT I WAS SO AFRAID OF ENDING UP BACK IN ANOTHER CAMP LIKE THE ONE I'D JUST LEFT, SO I WENT FOR IT.

WE TURNED THE FIRST CORNER AND THEN STARTED RUNNING.

?

WE STOPPED AFTER MAYBE TEN MINUTES.
ISZERHOLT
Ž
ŽATEC
PFF!
PFF!
WE'D BEEN EATING AND SLEEPING POORLY, SO WE WERE WEAK.

COME ON, LET'S GET SOMETHING TO EAT.
I NEED A MINUTE.

ÉLELMISZERHOLT
Ž
ŽATEC

1500 FORINTS, PLEASE.

OH, SORRY, I DON'T HAVE ANY HUNGARIAN MONEY.
NO PROBLEM!

DO YOU KNOW WHERE WE COULD GET A CAB TO BUDAPEST?

NO CAB WOULD AGREE TO TAKE YOU.
THE TOWN'S FULL OF SOLDIERS.

WELL, WHERE WOULD WE FIND SOME MEANS OF GETTING TO BUDAPEST?
THE STATION.
THAT'S IT.

MAYBE WE SHOULDN'T HAVE LEFT.
WE MIGHT END UP STUCK HERE.
ISZERHOLT
ŽATEC

WE'VE STILL GOT 45 MINUTES UNTIL THE TRAIN LEAVES.
THERE'S STILL TIME TO GO BACK.

WHAT'S THE WORST THAT COULD HAPPEN, REALLY?
THEY'LL JUST SEND US BACK TO THE CAMP.

TO ME, THAT WAS UNTHINKABLE.

AND THEN WE RAN INTO SOMEONE WHO, TO THIS DAY, I THANK HEAVEN THAT WE MET.

HEY, GUYS!
ARE YOU MIGRANTS?

Y- YES, WE'RE SYRIAN.
I'M GOING TO LUXEMBOURG.

FRANCE FOR ME.

NICE TO MEET YOU, I'M DIDIER.
FROM CÔTE D'IVOIRE.

I USED TO BE A MIGRANT, LIKE YOU.

I LEFT MY COUNTRY 10 YEARS AGO.
I WAS ALSO PLANNING TO GO TO FRANCE.
AND THEN I SETTLED HERE IN HUNGARY.
I'M DOING WELL. I RECENTLY GAINED NATIONALITY.
I HAVE A GOOD JOB, I'M A P.E. TEACHER.

WHY DON'T YOU STAY HERE?
I HAVE TO GET TO MY GIRLFRIEND.
AND MY WIFE.

WELL, IF IT'S FOR LOVE, I GUESS IT'S WORTH IT!!
HAHA!

DO YOU KNOW WHERE WE CAN FIND A CAB?
WE WANT TO GET TO BUDAPEST.

A CAB?
IN YOUR SITUATION, IT'S TRICKY...

I HAVE A FRIEND WHO'S A DRIVER. I'LL SEE WHAT HE SAYS.
TAP! TAP!

HELLO, SANDOR?
HOW ARE YOU?
OK, SO I'M WITH THESE TWO GUYS, MIGRANTS, AND THEY WANT TO GET TO BUDAPEST.
COULD YOU TAKE THEM?

DO THEY HAVE PAPERS?
NO.
NO.
DID YOU HEAR?

PLEASE! THEY'VE GOT A LITTLE KID WITH THEM. THEY'RE STUCK HERE.

MMM...
UNDERSTOOD, UNDERSTOOD.
NO WORRIES.
TALK TO YOU LATER!

HE SAYS IT'S TOO RISKY.
HE DOESN'T WANT ANY TROUBLE WITH THE LAW.

PFF... WHAT DO WE DO NOW?
OH, BUT HE GAVE ME THE NUMBER OF A GUY WHO DOES UNDER-THE-TABLE TRANSPORT.
TAP!
TAP!
WE'LL SEE WHAT HE SAYS.

IT WAS OUR LAST CHANCE...
IF THIS DIDN'T WORK, WE'D HAVE TO GO BACK TO THE TRAIN STATION.

WELL?
HE SEEMS OK. HE'LL BE HERE IN 30.

WOW, YOU'RE SUCH A STRONG BOY!
HEEHEE!
DO YOU LIFT?

ARE YOU DIDIER?
YES, HELLO!

OK...
RIGHT NOW, THINGS ARE A LITTLE DICEY. THE POLICE ARE EVERYWHERE.

WE HAVE TO WAIT UNTIL NIGHTFALL.
UNTIL THEN, I'LL BRING YOU SOMEWHERE MORE DISCREET.
IT'LL BE €200 PER PERSON.

THAT WORK FOR YOU?
SURE THING.
YES.
WE DIDN'T HAVE MUCH CHOICE.

THANKS SO MUCH, DIDIER!
NO PROBLEM!
AND I HOPE YOU'LL BE WITH YOUR LADY LOVES SOON!

WE DROVE THROUGH TOWN.

AND THE DRIVER STOPPED IN FRONT OF A PARK FAR FROM THE TOWN CENTER.

GO FIND SOMEWHERE QUIET TO WAIT.
I'LL BE BACK AT NIGHTFALL.

THERE WEREN'T MANY PEOPLE IN THE PARK.

JUST A YOUNG COUPLE.

MAN, I'VE BEEN AWAY FROM MY GIRLFRIEND TOO LONG.
I FEEL THE SAME WAY!

LET'S SIT ON THAT BENCH.
THAT BUSH WILL GIVE US SOME COVER.

COOKIE?
I WON'T SAY NO.
YOU TOO, KIDDO?

CRCH!
CRCH!
CRCH!
CRCH!

BY THE WAY, I'M AHMED!
HAKIM.
AND HADI.

*A CITY IN NORTHERN SYRIA.

IT WAS THE FIRST TIME I'D MET A REFUGEE WHO TALKED ABOUT OUR SITUATION FROM THIS ANGLE. HIS PERSPECTIVE ON IT SEEMED COMPREHENSIVE AND FAIR.

I'VE EVEN HEARD POLITICIANS SAYING THAT WE'RE COWARDS.
THAT WE SHOULD TAKE UP ARMS TO DEFEND OUR COUNTRY.

BUT FOR WHO?
THOSE ISIS BARBARIANS?
OR THE BUTCHERS IN POWER?

AND I'D LIKE TO KNOW WHAT KIND OF ARMS THEY WANT ME TO TAKE UP AGAINST BOMBS AND CHEMICAL WEAPONS...

I'M SURE IF ALL THIS WAS HAPPENING IN THEIR COUNTRIES, THEY'D BE THE FIRST TO FLEE.

OR WORSE, TO TAKE ADVANTAGE OF THE SITUATION TO TURN A PROFIT.

IT MUST HAVE BEEN HARD, WITH YOUR KID.
YOU COULD SAY THAT.

AND I DON'T THINK IT'S OVER YET.

OK, WHAT'S OUR DRIVER PLAYING AT?

WE SHOULD HAVE GOTTEN HIS NUMBER.
PFFF...

PLUS IT'S FREEZING.
FROT!
FROT!
FROT!

OK, COME ON.
LET'S GO!
SHOULDN'T WE WAIT A LITTLE LONGER?

WE'D DO BETTER TO FIND A PLACE TO SLEEP.
BESIDES, WHO KNOWS, THAT BASTARD COULD HAVE TURNED US IN.

HEY!

FINALLY! YOU TOOK YOUR TIME!!
YOU SAID YOU'D BE HERE AT "NIGHTFALL"!
IT'S BEEN NIGHT FOR 2 HOURS!!

THERE WERE SOLDIERS ALL OVER.
I TRIED TO WAIT AS LONG AS POSSIBLE.

NOW, IT'LL BE LESS RISKY.

INSH'ALLAH!

THE TRIP TO BUDAPEST LASTED A LITTLE MORE THAN 2 HOURS.
THE DRIVER TOOK ONLY BACK ROADS, AND AS HE DROVE HE MADE PHONE CALLS TO MAKE SURE THERE WERE NO POLICE ON OUR ROUTE.

HERE, TOO, I SAW THE SAME SCENES FROM EARLIER IN MY JOURNEY, BUT ON A MUCH LARGER SCALE.

THE STATION HAD BECOME A MASSIVE REFUGEE CAMP.

*QUOTES FROM RTL RADIO, 8/30/2015, PHILIPPE ROBUCHON & FOREIGN CORRESPONDENTS

A HUGE CROWD OF HUNDREDS OF PEOPLE WAS TRYING TO GET THROUGH THE LINE OF POLICE TO REACH THE PLATFORMS.
COOL IT!
GET BACK!!

BUT I HAVE A TICKET!
GET BACK, NO TRAINS ARE LEAVING TODAY!

OK...
I'M STILL GONNA GIVE IT A TRY...

I'M VERY GLAD I GOT TO MEET YOU, HAKIM.
GOOD LUCK ON YOUR JOURNEY.

YES, YOU TOO.

IT WAS 10 P.M., HADI WAS VERY TIRED, AND I TOLD MYSELF IT WAS BETTER TO WAIT UNTIL THE NEXT DAY RATHER THAN THROW MYSELF INTO THE FRAY.
C-D
A-B

I LEFT TO GO LOOK FOR SOME FOOD.

HI THERE, COULD I HAVE A LITTLE WATER AND SOMETHING TO EAT?

WHAT A SHAME!
GO FIND SOME WORK! YOU SHOULD PAY FOR THINGS RATHER THAN BEGGING.

DON'T MIND HIM.
WE KNOW WHY YOU'RE HERE.

WOULD YOU ALSO LIKE A BOTTLE OF MILK FOR YOUR LITTLE ONE?
THAT'D BE GREAT.

OK, JUST ONE MOMENT.

HERE!
THANKS.

WHAT'S GOING ON HERE?
WHY SO MANY PEOPLE?
WHY CAN'T THEY GET ON THE TRAINS?

THE PRESIDENT CLOSED THE BORDERS.
CURRENTLY, MIGRANTS ARE NOT ALLOWED IN OR OUT OF THE COUNTRY.

BUT THE EU IS APPLYING PRESSURE AND WE'RE HOPING HE'LL REOPEN THINGS.

REFUGEES ARE PILING UP HERE. THE SITUATION IS GETTING TENSE.

THE MIGRANTS ARE PROTESTING, THE LOCALS ARE FED UP, THE POLICE ARE OVERWHELMED.
THINGS ARE COMING TO A HEAD.

THEN WHY DON'T ALL THESE PEOPLE LEAVE VIA OTHER METHODS, RATHER THAN WAITING FOR A TRAIN?
YOU CAN'T LEAVE THE AREA AROUND THE STATION.

I DON'T KNOW IF YOU SAW, BUT THERE ARE POLICE ALL AROUND. THEY'RE KEEPING YOU HERE.
RIGHT NOW, YOU'RE BEING FORCED TO STAY HERE AND WAIT.

BUT DON'T GIVE UP HOPE. EVENTUALLY THEY'LL GIVE UP AND LET YOU LEAVE...

LET'S GO DOWN TO THE SUBWAY TO WARM UP, HADI.

IN THERE, TOO, WERE HUNDREDS AND HUNDREDS OF REFUGEES.
Keletipályaudvar

HAKIM!!

HAKIM!
OVER HERE!
NIHAD!!

SO GOOD TO SEE YOU AGAIN!
YOU SAID IT, BROTHER.

IT'S INCREDIBLE THAT WE FOUND EACH OTHER AGAIN, ESPECIALLY WITH ALL THESE PEOPLE!!
IT'S MAKTUB, HAKIM!

HAVE YOU BEEN HERE LONG?
I JUST GOT HERE.

WE SPENT 7 DAYS IN A CAMP.

THE SAME THING HAPPENED TO US...

WE'VE BEEN HERE FOR TWO DAYS.
THEY WON'T LET US GET ON THE TRAINS.

I JUST GOT IN CONTACT WITH A CAB DRIVER WHO CAN TAKE US TO THE AUSTRIAN BORDER.
IT'S A LOT MORE MONEY THAN THE TRAIN, BUT THIS WAY WE CAN ACTUALLY LEAVE.

HE'S PICKING US UP TOMORROW. DO YOU WANT TO COME ALONG?
IT'D BE €400 FOR YOU.

A LADY WITH THE RED CROSS TOLD ME WE COULDN'T LEAVE THE TRAIN STATION.
I'VE HEARD THAT TOO.
BUT I GUESS WE'LL SEE...

I ASKED MYSELF: WHAT WAS THE RISK IF WE WERE CAUGHT? WOULD WE BE SENT BACK TO A CAMP? I DIDN'T WANT TO GO THROUGH SOMETHING LIKE THAT AGAIN.
BESIDES, I ONLY HAD €650 LEFT TO FINISH MY JOURNEY. IF I SPENT €400 ON A CAB, I'D REALLY HAVE TO GET TO FRANCE QUICKLY.

CAN I THINK ABOUT IT AND LET YOU KNOW TOMORROW?
NO PROBLEM. DO WHAT YOU THINK IS BEST.

THAT NIGHT WAS REALLY HARD.

THE COLD, THE NOISE, THE LIGHT, THE STRESS.

AND THE THREATS...
GO BACK HOME!

A VISIBLY DRUNK HUNGARIAN MAN CONFRONTED SOME MIGRANTS.
WE DON'T WANT YOU HERE!!

YOU'RE TAKING ADVANTAGE OF US,
YOU LAZY SLOBS!

THE POLICE INTERVENED, BUT WE WERE ALL SHAKEN UP.
GOOD-FOR-NOTHINGS!!
WAAAH

BY MORNING, I'D MADE MY CHOICE.
I'M COMING WITH YOU.
I COULDN'T IMAGINE SPENDING ANOTHER NIGHT IN THOSE CONDITIONS.

I'M GLAD.

LET ME JUST CALL THE DRIVER TO CHECK IF THERE WILL BE ENOUGH SPACE.

IT'S OK?
PERFECT!
WHERE DO WE MEET?

THAT'S NEXT TO THE STATION?
GREAT, WE'LL SEE YOU SOON.

WE'RE OFF!
IT REMAINED TO BE SEEN HOW WE'D GET AWAY FROM THE STATION.

WHEN WE CAME OUT OF THE SUBWAY, HUNDREDS OF PEOPLE WERE RUNNING TOWARD THE DOORS TO THE STATION.

?

WHAT'S GOING ON?

THEY CHARTERED TWO TRAINS TO CLEAR PEOPLE OUT OF HERE.
ONE'S GOING TO GERMANY, THE OTHER AUSTRIA.

YOU STILL COMING WITH US?
YES, WITH THIS MANY PEOPLE, I DON'T KNOW IF I'D MAKE IT ON BOARD.

I CAN ALWAYS TRY THAT IF THE POLICE STOP US FROM LEAVING.

THEY LIFTED THE BLOCKADE.
YOU CAN LEAVE THE AREA IF YOU WANT.
IT WAS MORE THAN WE COULD HAVE HOPED FOR! (THOUGH IT DIDN'T MEAN THE HUNGARIAN GOVERNMENT WAS EASING UP ON MIGRANTS.)

SO WE SET OFF TO FIND OUR CAB.
THE STREET'S A LITTLE FARTHER UP, ON THE LEFT.

THERE HE IS!
férfi fodrasz

COME ON!
GET IN!

YOU OK?
NOT TOO TIGHT BACK THERE?
WE'RE OK.
GOOD, THE DRIVE'S ONLY AN HOUR AND A HALF ANYWAY.

I'LL GIVE YOU SOME ADVICE ALONG THE WAY.
AS YOU'VE SURELY NOTICED, PEOPLE IN HUNGARY HAVE PARTICULAR FEELINGS ABOUT REFUGEES RIGHT NOW.
ZÖLDSÉG-GYÜMÖLES
AND IT'S NOT BECAUSE THE POLICE LET YOU LEAVE THE STATION TODAY, OR BECAUSE THE POLITICS AROUND REFUGEES HAVE MELLOWED OUT.

ABOVE ALL, YOU MUST AVOID EXPOSING YOURSELVES.
YOU MUST BE DISCREET.

THERE ARE MANY HERE WHO DON'T LIKE PEOPLE LIKE YOU.
THEY WON'T HESITATE TO TURN YOU IN TO THE POLICE.

ALSO, AVOID ACCEPTING HELP FROM ANYONE.
THEY COULD TAKE ADVANTAGE OR STEAL FROM YOU.

I'M BRINGING YOU TO A TOWN ABOUT 20 KILOMETERS FROM THE BORDER.
I CAN'T GET ANY CLOSER WITHOUT RISKING A POLICE CHECKPOINT.

FROM THERE YOU'LL TAKE A BUS TO GET CLOSER TO THE BORDER.
WITHIN 5 KILOMETERS.

YOU'LL FINISH THE JOURNEY ON FOOT.
MAKE SURE YOU WALK UNDER COVER.

Bus Zállomás
OK, WE'RE HERE.
BUY YOUR TICKETS AND WAIT FOR THE BUS.
IT'S THE 512.

DON'T FORGET.
BE DISCREET.

VRRR

HELLO, WE'D LIKE 5 TICKETS FOR BUS 512, PLEASE.

HERE, IT LEAVES IN 3 HOURS.

I WONDERED IF IT WOULDN'T HAVE BEEN BETTER TO WAIT SOMEWHERE QUIET TO AVOID BEING SPOTTED.
GULP!

THEN...
WEEOO!
RENDŐRSÉG

IT SEEMED SOMEONE HAD CALLED THEM ON US.
GOOD DAY, FOLKS.
YOUR PAPERS, PLEASE.

THANKS.

NIHAD'S FAMILY'S PAPERS WERE, THEORETICALLY, IN ORDER, BUT I DIDN'T HAVE THE PASS I WAS SUPPOSED TO GET UPON LEAVING THE CAMP.

I TRIED TO APPEAR CALM, BUT ON THE INSIDE I WAS PANICKING.

HERE!
THANKS.

AND THEY LEFT.
WEEOO!
I THINK THEY WERE THE LOCAL POLICE AND THEY DIDN'T DEAL WITH MIGRANTS VERY OFTEN. MAYBE THEY HADN'T NOTICED ANYTHING WRONG...

THE BUS ARRIVED AROUND 3 P.M.
512 KÖZPON

AND 30 MINUTES LATER...
VRRR

WE REACHED OUR DESTINATION.

IT WAS A TINY LITTLE VILLAGE.

ACCORDING TO THE GPS, WE GO THROUGH THE CENTER OF TOWN.

BUT I'M NOT SURE IF IT'S A GOOD IDEA AFTER WHAT HAPPENED EARLIER.

HEY!

YOU'RE HEADED FOR AUSTRIA, RIGHT?

NO, NO.
NOT AT ALL.

OH, OK! THAT'S FINE!
ANYWAY, IF YOU EVER DO WANT TO HEAD THAT WAY, BE AWARE THERE ARE POLICE ALL OVER.

IT'S CALMER AROUND 9 P.M. THOUGH.

...
THANKS.
BUT WHAT WOULD WE DO WHILE WE WAIT?
IS THERE ANOTHER ROUTE?

THERE'S A LITTLE PARK OUTSIDE THE VILLAGE. YOU'LL BE SAFE THERE.
I SUGGEST YOU GO THERE AND WAIT.

WE'RE HUNGRY. DO YOU KNOW WHERE WE COULD GET SOMETHING TO EAT?

HMM...
THERE IS A LITTLE SHOP IN THE VILLAGE, BUT IT'S TOO RISKY.

AT MOST I COULD TAKE ONE. JUST YOU IN THE SCARF.
YOU COULD PASS FOR MY SON.

NO, NAWAL! DON'T GO!
WHAT IF SOMETHING HAPPENS?

NOTHING WILL HAPPEN TO ME, MOM. I'LL BE WITH THIS MAN.
DON'T YOU REMEMBER? THE CAB DRIVER TOLD US NOT TO ACCEPT ANY HELP.

WELL? WHAT DO YOU THINK?

GO! WE'LL SEE YOU AT THE PARK!
GET ENOUGH FOR US TO EAT AND DRINK FOR A FEW DAYS, IN CASE WE CAN'T RESUPPLY FOR A BIT.

WE SHOULDN'T HAVE LET HIM GO, NIHAD.
VRRR

I HAVE HIS PAPERS.
IF THEY RUN INTO TROUBLE, I'M CONFIDENT HE CAN CONVINCE THE POLICE THAT HE'S THAT MAN'S SON.

AND IF THE GUY'S A THIEF, THERE WON'T BE MUCH FOR HIM TO STEAL.
HE ONLY HAS ENOUGH MONEY FOR GROCERIES.
VRRR

I THINK HE'S A GOOD PERSON.
HE ONLY AGREED TO TAKE NAWAL BECAUSE WE ASKED HIM WHERE TO FIND FOOD.

IT WASN'T HIS IDEA.

I HOPE YOU'RE RIGHT...
VRRR

AFTER WE'D WALKED FOR 15 MINUTES, WE GOT TO THE LITTLE PARK THE MAN HAD TOLD US ABOUT.
VRRR

IT WAS AN AREA AT THE EDGE OF A FOREST.
IT WAS MORE OF A FIELD THAN A PARK, REALLY.

THE PLACE WAS DESERTED, AND IT WAS VERY COLD.

AND HALF AN HOUR AFTER WE GOT THERE, NAWAL ARRIVED WITH THE MAN.
VRRR

I GOT COOKIES, BREAD, AND WATER.
EXCELLENT.

AND YOU SHOULD CUT THROUGH THE FOREST, IT'S SAFER.
THERE ARE MORE POLICE THAN I EXPECTED IN THE VILLAGE.
I'D SUGGEST YOU LEAVE AT DAWN TOMORROW, NOT TONIGHT.

BUT HOW CAN WE SPEND THE NIGHT HERE? IT'S TOO COLD OUT!
CAN WE FIND A HOTEL NEARBY?

NO, THE CLOSEST IS THE TOWN WHERE YOU GOT ON THE BUS.
OH NO, WE'RE NOT GOING BACK THERE!

AND UNFORTUNATELY, I CAN'T RISK SHELTERING YOU FOR THE NIGHT.
IF I GET CAUGHT, I COULD BE IN SERIOUS TROUBLE.

WE UNDERSTAND...
IN ANY CASE, THANK YOU FOR WHAT YOU'VE DONE FOR US.

LISTEN...
WAIT HERE. I'LL GO GRAB YOU SOME STUFF TO GET YOU THROUGH THE NIGHT.

COFFEE, A LITTLE STOVE, BLANKETS.
IT WON'T BE ANYTHING LUXURIOUS, BUT AT LEAST YOU WON'T GET TOO COLD.

SEE YOU SOON!

WE WAITED. AND WAITED.

IT WAS GETTING COLDER AND COLDER.

NIGHT HAD FALLEN AND THE MAN STILL WASN'T BACK.
IN THAT MOMENT,
I WAS CERTAIN THAT I WAS ABOUT TO EXPERIENCE ONE OF THE WORST NIGHTS OF MY JOURNEY.

WHAT'S HE PLAYING AT?
IT'S ALREADY 10 O'CLOCK!

WE COULD LEAVE FOR AUSTRIA NOW. IT WOULD WARM US UP, AT LEAST.

YES, I AGREE WITH FADI.
BUT THE MAN SAID THE POLICE WERE ALL OVER.
WE SHOULD STAY HERE.

WHAT IF HE CALLED THE POLICE ON US?
THEY'LL COME AND TAKE US.

LISTEN!
LET'S GO A LITTLE DEEPER INTO THE FOREST TO HIDE.

WE'LL STAY FOR THE NIGHT AND HEAD OUT IN THE MORNING.
THAT OK, HAKIM?
YES.
NIHAD WAS RIGHT.
IT WAS THE LEAST RISKY SOLUTION.

RESIGNED, WE HEADED INTO THE FOREST.

THE COLD WAS GLACIAL. IT WAS PITCH BLACK.
MMM
BE BRAVE, HADI.

WE SAT DOWN AT THE BASE OF A TREE, HUDDLED TOGETHER TO GET THROUGH THE NIGHT.

CRRR
DID YOU HEAR THAT?

CRRR

WHAT IS IT?

NOTHING TO WORRY ABOUT, BOYS!
I'M SURE IT'S JUST THE TREES CREAKING.

ALMIGHTY ALLAH, PROTECT US, I PRAY.

BE CALM, MY DEAR, IT WILL BE ALRIGHT.

WAAAAH!

DON'T CRY, HADI. WE HAVE TO KEEP QUIET.
mmm

DAD, I'M SO COLD!
WE'RE GONNA DIE...
SHHH!

CHIN UP, IT'S JUST ONE NIGHT.
AND WE'RE TOGETHER. NOTHING BAD IS GOING TO HAPPEN TO US.

PLIC!

DAD!!
PLIC
IT'S RAINING. WE'LL FREEZE TO DEATH!!!
PLIC
PLIC

WAAA
AAH!

OOOOOOHHH
SNIFF! SNIFF!
THE WORST NIGHT OF MY JOURNEY, AS I SAID.

DESPITE THE COLD AND THE FEAR, I FINALLY FELL ASLEEP OUT OF EXHAUSTION.

I WOKE UP AROUND 4 A.M. THE OTHERS WERE SLEEPING.

EXCEPT NIHAD, WHO STARED STRAIGHT AHEAD...

NIHAD, YOU OK?

HEY!! NIHAD!!
HMMM?
YOU OK?

I HAVEN'T SLEPT. I'M FROZEN.
I CAN'T FEEL MY FINGERS, OR MY FEET.
AS SOON AS IT STARTS GETTING LIGHT, WE'LL GO.

AROUND 6 A.M., THE FIRST LIGHT OF DAY APPEARED.

COME ON, WE HAVE TO GET GOING.

THE GPS SAYS WE KEEP GOING THIS WAY.
OK, SWEETIE, LET'S GO.

WE CAN'T LINGER TOO LONG. MY PHONE IS ALMOST OUT OF BATTERY.

WE WALKED FOR A LITTLE OVER AN HOUR.

EVERYONE, STOP!

VRRRRRR
MOL

NOW DO WE FOLLOW THE ROAD?
I DON'T KNOW. MY BATTERY'S DEAD.

WE COULD ASK FOR DIRECTIONS AT THE SERVICE STATION?
THAT SEEMS RISKY TO ME.

LET'S GET CLOSER. THERE COULD BE SIGNS ON THE ROAD.
YES, GOOD IDEA.

VRRRR

VRRR

NO LUCK...

AND THEN WE SAW, OVER AT THE STATION, A TRUCK DRIVER WHO WAS WAVING AT US.
FRIGOR

YIKES! HE SAW US!
QUICK, LET'S GO!!

HANG ON...

HE KNEW WHAT WE NEEDED.
AND HE WAS SHOWING US THE WAY.

WE WALKED, HIDDEN BY THE TREES.
VRRR

VRRR
VRRR

LOOK!

COP CARS.
FROM WHERE WE WERE, IT WAS IMPOSSIBLE TO KNOW IF THEY WERE HUNGARIAN OR AUSTRIAN.

AND WE DIDN'T KNOW IF WE WERE LOOKING AT A BORDER CROSSING OR A SIMPLE TOLLBOOTH.

JUST IN CASE, WE DECIDED TO KEEP GOING IN THE SAME DIRECTION, STAYING EVEN FARTHER FROM THE ROAD.
VRRR

WE'RE PAST THAT BOOTH.
WE MIGHT ALREADY BE IN AUSTRIA.

LET'S KEEP GOING FOR A BIT, SO WE CAN BE REALLY SURE.

THIS WAY.

PUTT! PUTT!

PUTT!
PUTT!

PUTT!
PUTT!

HALLO!

H- HALLO.

PUTT!
PUTT!

HE SAID "HALLO"!
THAT'S GERMAN.
WE'RE IN AUSTRIA!!

WE'D MADE IT.
HAHA, WE DID IT! WE'RE IN AUSTRIA!

A WEIGHT LIFTED OFF OUR SHOULDERS.
HAHA!
HAHAHA!

WE WERE WORN OUT BUT RELIEVED.
WE MADE IT, DEAR.
ALLAH IS GREAT.

WELL DONE, BOYS, YOU WERE SO BRAVE!
WHAT AN ADVENTURE, BROTHER!

VRRRRR
?

VRRR

STAY CALM.
THE GUY ON THE TRACTOR MUST HAVE CALLED THEM ON US.
THE BASTARD!

POLIZEI

HELLO!
HELLO.

WOULD YOU PLEASE SHOW US YOUR PAPERS?
Y- YES.
POLIZEI

HERE.
THANKS.
HEY KIDDO, HOW OLD ARE YOU?

HE'S A YEAR AND A HALF.
WELL, HE'S REALLY CUTE.
TH- THANKS.
THE AUSTRIAN POLICE WERE REALLY VERY DIFFERENT FROM THE HUNGARIANS.

DON'T BE AFRAID.
WE'RE HERE TO HELP YOU.
POLIZEI

HERE YOU GO.
WE'RE CALLING A BUS TO COME PICK YOU UP.
POL

IT WILL TAKE YOU TO A TRANSIT CENTER.
A CAMP? LIKE IN HUNGARY?

NO, DON'T WORRY.
YOU WON'T BE THERE LONG AND YOU'LL BE TREATED WELL.

THERE YOU'LL BE GIVEN PASSES TO CONTINUE YOUR JOURNEY.
IF YOU'D LIKE.

WHILE ONE OF THE OFFICERS WENT TO CALL A BUS, THE OTHERS ASKED US A BUNCH OF QUESTIONS.
WHERE ARE YOU FROM?
HOW DID YOU ALL MAKE IT THIS FAR?
THEY WEREN'T TRYING TO INTERROGATE US. THEY WERE JUST KIND PEOPLE.

HERE'S THE BUS.
POLIZEI
POLIZEI
VRRR

SAFE TRAVELS.

GOODBYE, KIDDO.
I HOPE YOU GET TO SEE YOUR MOM SOON.
POLIZEI

Chapter 14: Austria and Switzerland (Late September 2015)

"I'M CALLING BECAUSE I'M IN VIENNA AND I NEED YOUR HELP."

ON THE BUS, THE ATMOSPHERE AMONG THE REFUGEES WAS LIGHTHEARTED.

PEOPLE WERE EVEN SMILING.

SOMETHING I'D RARELY SEEN SINCE LEAVING TURKEY.

EVERY PERSON ON THAT BUS HAD BEEN THROUGH DIFFICULT THINGS.

AND ALL OF US WERE RELIEVED TO HAVE MADE IT TO AUSTRIA.

I WAS SEATED NEXT TO A SYRIAN (HONESTLY, ALMOST ALL OF THE PASSENGERS WERE SYRIAN), AND WE TALKED A LITTLE BIT ABOUT OUR JOURNEYS.

ONE MORNING, AT THE BUDAPEST STATION, THEY CHARTERED TWO TRAINS.
ONE GOING TO GERMANY, THE OTHER AUSTRIA.
YES, I REMEMBER, I WAS THERE FOR THAT.

WHEN THEY MADE THE ANNOUNCEMENT, IT WAS MAYHEM, EVERYONE WANTED ON, ESPECIALLY SINCE THEY WERE TAKING PEOPLE WHO DIDN'T HAVE TICKETS.

I MANAGED TO GET ON BOARD.
I WAS RELIEVED.

THE TRAIN TRAVELED FOR A LITTLE WHILE, THEN STOPPED NEAR THE BORDER.
BUT STILL IN HUNGARY.
WHICH SEEMED STRANGE.

THEY REALLY JUST WANTED TO PUT US BACK IN CAMPS.
IT WAS ALL A TRICK TO CLEAR OUT THE STATION.

WE ALL PROTESTED AND THE POLICE WERE OVERWHELMED. THEY COULDN'T HOLD US.
I TOOK MY CHANCE AND RAN.

IT WAS LUCKY I'D GONE WITH NIHAD'S FAMILY.

AFTER A FEW MINUTES OF DRIVING, THE BUS CAME TO A TOWN.

AND IT STOPPED IN FRONT OF A BIG WAREHOUSE.

IT LOOKED LIKE A UTILITY SERVICE SITE.

A YOUNG VOLUNTEER GREETED US IN ARABIC.
WELCOME TO AUSTRIA!

YOU'RE HERE SO WE CAN REGISTER YOU AND GIVE YOU PAPERS TO SHOW YOU'RE IN GOOD STANDING.

YOU MUST TELL US IF YOU PLAN TO STAY IN AUSTRIA OR CONTINUE ON FROM HERE.
UNHCR

FOR THOSE CONTINUING ON, YOU CAN LEAVE ONCE YOU'RE GIVEN YOUR PASSES.
DON'T LEAVE BEFORE THEN, OR YOU'LL HAVE TROUBLE IF YOU ENCOUNTER A POLICE CHECKPOINT.

TO THOSE OF YOU WHO HAVE BEEN IN CAMPS IN HUNGARY, PLEASE DON'T WORRY.
WE DON'T WANT TO HOLD YOU HERE AND YOU'LL BE TREATED WELL.

THIS IS JUST TO GET YOUR STATUSES SORTED OUT.
TOMORROW AT THE LATEST, YOU'LL BE ABLE TO LEAVE.

WHILE YOU WAIT, YOU DON'T HAVE TO REMAIN IN THE WAREHOUSE.
YOU CAN GO DO SOME SHOPPING IN TOWN, IF YOU'D LIKE.

BUT I REPEAT: DO NOT LEAVE WITHOUT YOUR PASS.

NOW, FOLLOW ME!

YOU CAN TAKE ANY BED THAT'S FREE.
THE SHEETS ARE CLEAN.

OVER HERE, YOU CAN HELP YOURSELF TO TEA, COFFEE, AND SNACKS.

IT REALLY FELT LIKE WE WERE BEING TREATED LIKE PEOPLE WHO HAD VALUE.
UNLIKE IN HUNGARY, WHERE WE'D FELT LIKE ANIMALS OR CRIMINALS.

THIS FRIENDLY ATMOSPHERE HELPED US TO FEEL FREE OF THE STRESS OF THE LAST FEW MONTHS.

AND WE SPENT THE DAY CHATTING QUIETLY.

IN LATE AFTERNOON, A PERSON FROM IMMIGRATION SERVICES CAME TO REGISTER OUR REQUESTS.
YOUR NAME?
HAKIM KABDI.
AND HADI KABDI.
HE'S MY SON.

DO YOU HAVE IDENTITY DOCUMENTS?
YES, HERE.

WHICH WOULD YOU LIKE?
AN ASYLUM REQUEST OR A PASS?
A PASS.

ALRIGHT, HERE ARE YOUR PAPERS.
THANKS.

TOMORROW, IF YOU'D LIKE, A BUS WILL TAKE YOU TO THE TRAIN STATION.

NEXT.
THERE WERE A LOT OF US. IT TOOK UNTIL 9 P.M. TO FINISH REGISTERING US.

WE WERE ALL IN GOOD SPIRITS, AND I TALKED WITH NIHAD AND HIS FAMILY UNTIL MIDNIGHT.
SO? WHERE EXACTLY IN GERMANY ARE YOU GOING?

DORTMUND.
A BIG CITY IN THE NORTH.
THEY HAVE A GREAT SOCCER TEAM!

THAT'S NOT WHY WE PICKED IT.
HAHA!
IT'S MAINLY BECAUSE I HAVE A COUSIN WHO LIVES THERE.

IF ALL GOES WELL, WE'LL BE THERE IN 2 OR 3 DAYS.

AND YOU?
AIX-EN-PROVENCE.

BUT THEY DON'T HAVE A SOCCER TEAM.
HAHA!
HAHA!

THAT NIGHT, FOR THE FIRST TIME IN A VERY LONG WHILE, I WAS ABLE TO SLEEP DEEPLY AND PEACEFULLY.

WHEN I WOKE UP, IT WAS LATE.

THE WAREHOUSE WAS ALMOST EMPTY AND NEW MIGRANTS WERE COMING IN.
FOLLOW ME!

EVEN NIHAD AND HIS FAMILY HAD LEFT.

I WAS A LITTLE DISAPPOINTED, BUT AS I'VE SAID BEFORE, WE WERE TRAVEL COMPANIONS WHO SHARED A COMMON GOAL.
UP WE GET, SWEETHEART!
NOT FRIENDS WHO WERE ON VACATION TOGETHER.

THOUGH, TO TELL THE TRUTH, A FEW DAYS LATER, NIHAD WROTE TO ME AND EXPLAINED THAT THEY'D LEFT ON THE FIRST BUS AROUND 4 A.M. AND HADN'T WANTED TO WAKE ME.
THEY THOUGHT WE NEEDED TO RECOVER. THEY WEREN'T WRONG.

HELLO, WHERE IS THE BUS TO THE STATION?

THERE AREN'T ANY MORE TODAY.
RIGHT NOW THEY'RE OUT PICKING UP OTHER REFUGEES TO BRING THEM HERE.

BUT THE STATION'S ONLY 2 KILOMETERS AWAY.
YOU CAN WALK IF YOU LIKE.

I TOOK A FEW COOKIES FOR THE ROAD AND I LEFT.

HELLO!
HELLO!

ARE YOU HUNGRY? THIRSTY?
NO THANKS, I'M OK.

WHAT ABOUT HIM?
DOES YOUR BOY WANT ANYTHING?
NO, REALLY, IT'S FINE.

WAIT JUST A SEC.

?

HERE!

DIAPERS.
THEY'RE MY GRANDSON'S.
OH, THANKS! I'D RUN OUT.

HAVE A CANDY, TOO.
FANK!

BAHNHOF
ÖBB

AT THE STATION, PEOPLE HELPED ME FIND A TRAIN TO VIENNA.
YOU SHOULD GET ON THIS ONE.
THANKS!
ÖBB

I CAN FINALLY GET YOU BACK IN DIAPERS, HADI.

BUT STILL LET ME KNOW IF YOU NEED TO GO TO THE BATHROOM, OK?
ÖBB

WE REACHED VIENNA IN LATE MORNING.
Wien Hauptbahnhof
ÖBB

THE STATION WAS HUGE.
TELEKO
SPORT
IN OUT

I WANDERED AROUND, WONDERING HOW TO FIND A TRAIN TO FRANCE.
OPTIKER

AUSGAN
BREUER
ANKE

HEY, YOU!
OHLER
MY FIRST INSTINCT WAS TO BE AFRAID EVEN THOUGH MY PAPERS WERE IN ORDER.

WHEN YOU'RE USED TO HIDING FROM PEOPLE IN UNIFORM, YOU DEVELOP A KIND OF INTRINSIC FEAR.
COME OVER HERE! DON'T BE AFRAID!

YES?
ARE YOU LOOKING FOR SOMETHING?

NO, I'M FINE.
DON'T WORRY, IT'S OK.
I IMAGINE YOU'VE BEEN THROUGH A LOT TO GET HERE.
COULD I PERHAPS HELP?

I'M LOOKING FOR A TRAIN TO FRANCE.
OK.
POLIZE

THIS WAY!

HE BROUGHT ME TO AN UNDERGROUND CONCOURSE WHERE MAYBE 200 OR 300 REFUGEES WERE WAITING.

OVER THERE YOU CAN MEET WITH PEOPLE FROM THE ASSOCIATION.
THEY'LL TELL YOU EVERYTHING YOU NEED TO KNOW.
WIENER RO
KRE
POLIZEI
THEY EVEN HAVE DOCTORS, IF YOU NEED ONE.

IF YOU'RE GOING TO BERLIN, FOLLOW ME!

HELLO, SIR, I'M LOOKING FOR A TRAIN TO AIX-EN-PROVENCE.
ALRIGHT, LET'S SEE WHAT WE CAN DO FOR YOU.

KHADIJAH, CAN YOU TAKE THIS YOUNG MAN TO THE TICKET WINDOW?
HE WANTS TO GO TO AIX-EN-PROVENCE.
NO PROBLEM.

ARE YOU ALRIGHT? NOT TOO TIRED?
A BIT.
BUT I'M OK.

IS HE YOUR SON?
YES.
HE'S CUTE.
ÖBB
TICKETS
REIS

TICKETS
OK, LET'S SEE IF WE CAN FIND YOU A TRAIN.
HOW NICE, THANKS.

HELLO, MA'AM, CAN YOU TELL ME WHEN THE NEXT TRAIN TO AIX-EN-PROVENCE IS LEAVING?

HMM...
THERE AREN'T ANY.

WHAT ABOUT FRANCE?
I'LL LOOK.

THERE'S A TRAIN TO PARIS LEAVING AT 10 P.M.
WITH A CONNECTION IN ZURICH, SWITZERLAND.

WHAT DO YOU THINK?
FROM PARIS, YOU CAN TAKE A TRAIN TO AIX-EN-PROVENCE.
SURE, IF THAT'S THE ONLY OPTION...

HOW MUCH IS THE TICKET?
€240.
I'D SPENT A BIT OF MONEY SINCE BUDAPEST AND I DIDN'T HAVE ENOUGH.

ÖBB
REIS
DO YOU HAVE ANY FRIENDS OR FAMILY WHO COULD LEND YOU A LITTLE MONEY?

I DO HAVE AN UNCLE WHO LIVES IN VIENNA.
BUT I'D HATE TO ASK THAT OF HIM.
AND TRUTH BE TOLD, I'D BEEN SO FOCUSED ON MY GOAL THAT I HADN'T THOUGHT TO TELL HIM I WAS COMING THROUGH.

YOU HAVE TO CALL.
IF YOU'D LIKE, I CAN GIVE YOU A PHONE CARD.

WITH HER HELP, I FOUND MY UNCLE'S PHONE NUMBER AND CALLED HIM.
RIING RIING

HELLO?
HELLO, AMMI?*
IT'S YOUR NEPHEW HAKIM.
HAKIM!!! HOW ARE YOU?

I'M CALLING BECAUSE I'M IN VIENNA AND I NEED YOUR HELP.
?
IN VIENNA??!!

*UNCLE.

HE WAS SURPRISED, AND WANTED TO COME RIGHT AWAY TO PICK ME UP AT THE STATION AND TAKE ME TO HIS HOUSE.
ÖBB
HAHA!

IF YOU'D LIKE, YOU CAN STAY AT THE HOUSE FOR THREE OR FOUR DAYS TO REST UP.
YOU LOOK EXHAUSTED!

THAT'S THOUGHTFUL, BUT I'D RATHER GO AS SOON AS I CAN.
OF COURSE. I UNDERSTAND.

IN ANY CASE, I'LL GIVE YOU THE MONEY, IT'S NO PROBLEM!
IN FACT I'M GLAD TO!
WOW! I NEVER WOULD HAVE THOUGHT TO SEE MY NEPHEW TODAY.

AND I GET TO MEET HIS SON!
HAHA!!

THIS UNCLE WAS MY FATHER'S BROTHER. HE WAS 67 AND HAD MOVED TO AUSTRIA SHORTLY AFTER ALL THIS BEGAN.
LOKAL HOTEL
IN SYRIA, HE'D BEEN RICH. HE OWNED TWO NURSERIES AND, LIKE ME, HE'D LOST IT ALL.

MARAM! LOOK WHO'S HERE!!

HAKiiiiM!!
AMMTi,* iT'S SO GOOD TO SEE YOU!

*AUNTIE.

AND iS THIS YOUR SON?
YES, HiS NAME'S HADi.

HAKiM, DO YOU RECOGNiZE YOUR COUSiNS OSAMA AND MOAYAD?

WOW! YOU'VE GOTTEN SO BiG!!
Hi, HAKiM!

WHERE ARE THE REST OF THEM?
i HOPE THEY'RE ALRiGHT?
THEY HAD 10 KiDS...

THEY'RE WELL, THANK ALLAH.
BUT THEY'RE OF AGE SO THEY WEREN'T ALLOWED TO JOIN US HERE.

COME NOW, LET'S SIT DOWN. YOU MUST BE TIRED.
WE'LL GET SOME FOOD FOR YOU AND YOUR BOY.

WE SPENT THE REST OF THE AFTERNOON TALKING ABOUT MY JOURNEY, SYRIA, AND THEIR LIFE IN AUSTRIA.

THEY HADN'T SEEN THEIR OTHER CHILDREN SINCE THEY'D COME HERE, AND THIS WAS REALLY AFFECTING THEM.

THEY WERE TOO OLD TO WORK SO THEY LIVED ON WELFARE BENEFITS.

BUT THEY FELT THAT BY STAYING HERE, THEY WERE GIVING THEIR TWO YOUNGEST CHILDREN A CHANCE AT A REAL FUTURE.

PLUS, THE OLDER ONE HAD JUST RECEIVED A SCHOLARSHIP TO ATTEND THE UNIVERSITY OF VIENNA, AND THEY WERE VERY PROUD.

I GOT TO SHAVE AND TAKE A SHOWER, AND IN THE EARLY EVENING HE TOOK ME BACK TO THE STATION.
SEE YOU, AMMTI.

GOODBYE, BOYS.
AND GOOD LUCK WITH YOUR STUDIES.
THANKS.

SAFE TRAVELS, HAKIM.
ÖBB
ONCE YOU'RE SETTLED IN FRANCE, COME BACK AND SEE US. WE'RE NOT FAR.
WIEN HAUPTBAHNHOF
I WILL!

HERE, FOR YOUR TICKET.
THANKS, AMMI.

ON THE WAY TO MY TRAIN, I LOOKED AT THE PEOPLE AROUND ME.
↑ 9-10

I THOUGHT ABOUT THEM GOING TO WORK, OR TO SEE FAMILY OR FRIENDS.

IN THAT MOMENT, I REALIZED THAT IT HAD BEEN MONTHS, YEARS EVEN, SINCE I'D LIVED IN THE SAME WORLD AS THEM.
90 SHOPS

I DON'T KNOW HOW TO EXPLAIN THIS FEELING, BUT IT WAS LIKE I WAS IN A PARALLEL UNIVERSE.

AND I COULDN'T WAIT TO GET BACK TO REAL LIFE, TO BE ON MY WAY TO WORK, MY FAMILY, MY FRIENDS.

FOR TOO LONG I'D BEEN RUNNING AFTER SOMETHING THAT ELUDED ME.

SHHHH
ØBB
ØBB

SHHHH
ØBB

WE RODE ALL NIGHT.
WE WERE TO ARRIVE AT 7:30 A.M., IF I REMEMBER CORRECTLY.

BUT AROUND 6:30, THE TRAIN STOPPED IN A FREIGHT YARD.
?

EXCUSE ME, DO YOU KNOW IF WE'RE IN SWITZERLAND YET?
YES.
BUT WE HAVEN'T REACHED ZURICH.

PFFF... WHAT'S GOING ON?
I REALLY CAN'T MISS MY CONNECTION!

POLIZEI
POLIZEI

HELLO, SHOW ME YOUR PAPERS, PLEASE!

THANKS!
POLIZ

OLIZEI
PAPERS, PLEASE.

SIR, YOU'LL HAVE TO COME WITH ME.

WHO, ME?
B- BUT WHY?
IT'LL BE BETTER FOR EVERYONE IF YOU DON'T MAKE A FUSS.

POLIZ
POLIZEI

ÖBB
THEY'D BROUGHT AROUND TEN MIGRANTS DOWN ONTO THE PLATFORM.

THEY STARTED SEARCHING US.
WAAAH

IS THIS YOUR SON?
YES.
CAN YOU MAKE HIM STOP?

COME ON, SWEETIE, IT'S OK, CALM DOWN.
WAAAAH
HE WAS SCARED, AND HIS DIAPER WAS FULL.

DESTINATION?
FRANCE.

WHY?
MY WIFE LIVES THERE.
WAAAAH!

WHERE'S YOUR FRENCH VISA?
I DON'T HAVE ONE.
WAAAH!

BUT YOU SAID YOUR WIFE LIVES THERE.
YES, I'M JOINING HER.
AND SHE HAS A VISA?
YES.
WAAAAH

YOU'RE COMING WITH US. YOU CAN'T STAY ON THIS TRAIN.
WE'LL GET THIS ALL CLEARED UP.

WAIT, LET ME GO, I'M BEGGING YOU!!
I HAVE TO GET TO MY WIFE!

TRiiiiiiiii!
ÖBB

WAAAAAAH

WAAAAAH

WAAAAAH

WAAAAAH

?

WAAAAAH

SHHHH

TO THIS DAY, I DON'T REALLY UNDERSTAND WHAT HAPPENED.

I DON'T KNOW IF THEY FELT BAD.

OR IF MAYBE THEY DIDN'T WANT TO HAVE TO DEAL WITH A REFUGEE WITH A BABY.
SNIFF! SNIFF!

ESPECIALLY WITH A DIAPER THAT SMELLED OF POOP, HAHA!
OK, COME ON.
LET'S SIT DOWN.
SNIFF!
SNIFF!

IN ANY CASE, I COULDN'T CHANGE HIM.
WHEN I GOT BACK ON THE TRAIN, I ENDED UP IN A DIFFERENT CAR, AND MY BAG WAS STILL AT MY OLD SEAT.

I WAS SO SHAKEN UP BY WHAT HAD JUST HAPPENED THAT I DIDN'T WANT TO GO BACK AND FIND IT.

I SANK INTO THE FIRST OPEN SEAT THAT I FOUND.

AND I DIDN'T MOVE AGAIN UNTIL THE TRAIN ARRIVED.

AT THE STATION IN ZURICH, THERE WERE A LOT OF POLICE.
B
BB

I HAD AN HOUR TO KILL BEFORE MY TRAIN LEFT FOR PARIS.

SO I WENT AND SAT IN A CORNER OF THE STATION, AND I DIDN'T MOVE AGAIN UNTIL IT WAS TIME TO LEAVE.

WHEN MY TRAIN ARRIVED, AS I WALKED TO THE PLATFORM, I PRAYED NOT TO RUN INTO ANY POLICE.

TGV
AND THERE I WAS! GETTING ON THE TRAIN TO FRANCE!

THE CAR WAS FULL OF PEOPLE TRAVELING FOR WORK.

WITH THEIR SUITS AND LAPTOPS...

I STOOD OUT A LITTLE.

SHHHH
SNCF

HEY, LOOK, HONEY!

WE JUST CROSSED THE BORDER.

WE'RE IN FRANCE.

Chapter 15:
France
(Late September 2015)

"I LEFT HOME ALMOST 3 YEARS AGO."

LADIES AND GENTLEMEN, WELCOME TO PARIS GARE DE LYON...

I HAD NO BAG, AND ALMOST NO MONEY...

MY PHONE BATTERY WAS DEAD.

AND I DIDN'T KNOW HOW TO GET TO AIX-EN-PROVENCE.

BUT WE'D MADE IT. WE WERE IN FRANCE.

JUST A FEW HOURS AWAY FROM NAJMEH.

EVEN SO, I STILL WASN'T COMPLETELY RELAXED...
Hall 1 H
Kate Winslet
LA COLLECTION RECORD
LONGINES
TRAINS AU DÉPART
BRIOCHE DORÉE
I HOPED NOTHING BAD WOULD HAPPEN BEFORE I SAW HER.

HELLO!
DO YOU SPEAK ARABIC?

4€
YES, I'M ALGERIAN.
WHAT DO YOU NEED?

I'M SYRIAN, AND I GOT HERE FROM TURKEY...
WHOAAA!
THAT'S A HELL OF A TRIP!

YOU COULD SAY THAT...
I LEFT HOME ALMOST 3 YEARS AGO...

WOW!
DO YOU NEED ANYTHING?

I HAVE TO CALL MY FAMILY WHO LIVE IN THE SOUTH OF FRANCE. COULD YOU LEND ME A PHONE?
YES, OF COURSE!

HERE, BROTHER!

IT WAS NAJMEH'S FATHER WHO ANSWERED.
HELLO? ABDERRAHIM?
Brioche
WHO'S THIS?

IT'S ME, HAKIM!
HAKIM?
WHERE ARE YOU?

PARIS.
...

HAHAHA!
THANK HEAVENS!!
4€
6€
€
HAHAHA!
Brioche Dorée
WHEN DO YOU GET IN?

I DON'T KNOW YET.
HOW DO I GET TO AIX-EN-PROVENCE FROM HERE?
WHERE ARE YOU, EXACTLY?

THE GARE DE LYON.
AN ALGERIAN GUY IS LETTING ME USE HIS PHONE.

PASS ME TO HIM!

HERE, IT'S MY FATHER-IN-LAW.
HE WANTS TO TALK.

HELLO?
HELLO, COULD YOU HELP MY SON-IN-LAW BUY A TICKET TO AIX-EN-PROVENCE? HE DOESN'T KNOW WHAT TO DO.

Y- YEAH, NO PROBLEM.
THANK YOU SO MUCH, BLESS YOU.

AND TELL HIM TO CALL ME BACK WHEN HE KNOWS WHAT TIME HE'S GETTING IN.
I'LL PICK HIM UP.
OK.

COME WITH ME!
WE'RE BUYING YOUR TICKET.

MOUSSA, I'LL BE BACK IN 5.
OK.

EARLIEST POSSIBLE DEPARTURE?
YES.

GIVE ME YOUR CARD.
MY WHAT?
MY PASSPORT?

NO, A PAYMENT CARD.
A CREDIT CARD.
I DON'T HAVE ONE.

THEN HOW ARE YOU GONNA PAY?
IT ONLY TAKES CARDS.

CAN YOU PAY WITH YOUR CARD AND I'LL GIVE YOU THIS?
!
I THINK IT'S ENOUGH.

SURE, SINCE YOU'VE TRAVELED SO FAR TO GET HERE.
THANKS!

THE TRAIN WAS IN 2 HOURS.

i HAD A LiTTLE MONEY LEFT TO BUY DiAPERS AND COOKiES.
Monop' daily

AND BEFORE WE SAW NAJMEH, i WANTED US TO BE PRESENTABLE, TO SMELL NiCE.

WE'LL GET YOU NiCE AND CLEAN, KiDDO.

FOR THE FIRST TIME SINCE WE'D LEFT, I NOTICED HOW MUCH WE'D BEEN PHYSICALLY AFFECTED.
UNTIL THAT POINT—FUELED BY FEAR, ADRENALINE, AND THE WILL TO SUCCEED—I HADN'T PAID THIS ANY ATTENTION.

HADI'S LITTLE FEET WERE COVERED IN BLISTERS.

HE WAS VERY THIN.

THERE WERE BAGS UNDER HIS EYES.

THERE WAS STILL A LITTLE TIME LEFT BEFORE OUR DEPARTURE, SO I WENT OUTSIDE TO SMOKE.
GARE DE LYON
AND TO GET A GOOD LOOK AT THE COUNTRY THAT I'D BEEN TRYING TO REACH FOR SO LONG.

I SAW A HIVE OF ACTIVITY: EVERYONE SEEMED TO BE IN A HURRY, RUNNING EVERY WHICH WAY WITHOUT TALKING OR LOOKING AT EACH OTHER BUT STILL MANAGING NOT TO RUN INTO EACH OTHER.

I ALSO THOUGHT IT WAS BEAUTIFUL TO SEE THE ETHNIC MIXTURE THERE, UNLIKE ANY I'D SEEN.
LYON

AND THEN I THOUGHT I SAW THE EIFFEL TOWER OVERLOOKING THE CITY, LIKE A MOUNTAIN, BUT I WAS WRONG, HAHA!

OK, WE'RE OFF!
WE'RE GOING TO MAMA!
MAMA?

7

HELLO.
HELLO.

COULD YOU LET ME KNOW WHEN WE GET TO AIX-EN-PROVENCE?
OF COURSE!

MY EXCITEMENT AND STRESS GREW AS WE GOT CLOSER.

SIR.
YES?

WE'RE HERE.

WHEN THE TRAIN STOPPED, I RUSHED THROUGH THE DOORS.
TGV

I WAS SO AFRAID THAT IT WOULD LEAVE BEFORE I COULD GET OFF.

HAKIM!!

HAHAHAHA!!

AND NAJMEH?
WHERE IS SHE?

SHE HAD SOMETHING COME UP.

WHAT DO YOU MEAN?

HAKIM!

HAHA!
MY LOVE, YOU'RE HERE!!
I WANTED TO SURPRISE YOU!

YOU'RE FINALLY HERE! HAHA!
HAHA!
IT'S BEEN SUCH A LONG TIME!
I'VE MISSED YOU SO MUCH!
MMM, YOU SMELL GOOD, SWEETIE!
I'M GOING TO HAVE TO FATTEN YOU UP. YOU'RE SO SKINNY!
HAHA!
YOU'VE GOTTEN SO BIG, HONEY!
AND SO HANDSOME!

LET YOUR MAMA HOLD YOU!!
HE'S TIRED!
BUT DON'T WORRY!
SOON HE'LL BE SHOWERING YOU WITH KISSES!

SHALL WE?

YES, LET'S GO HOME.

NOW WE'RE TOGETHER!
FOREVER!

I CAN'T BELIEVE IT! WE'RE DONE!!
CAN YOU BELIEVE IT? WE'VE BEEN MEETING FOR A YEAR AND A HALF!

NOW WE'LL SEE WHAT YOU MAKE OF ALL THAT!
I HAVE A BIT OF WORK AHEAD OF ME.

SERIOUSLY, THANK YOU SO MUCH FOR YOUR PATIENCE AND YOUR TRUST.
IT WAS A PLEASURE.
WHEN THE BOOK'S READY, I'LL SEND IT TO YOU.
CLICK

HELLO, FABIEN.
OH! YOU'RE AWAKE.

WE JUST FINISHED. HE'S ABOUT TO LEAVE.
REALLY?

MY THANKS TO ALL OF YOU. YOU'RE A LOVELY FAMILY.
AND IF YOU EVER NEED ANYTHING, DON'T HESITATE TO CALL ME.

KING GRILL

"HAKIM'S ODYSSEY" REALLY COULD HAVE ENDED THERE.

IT'S TRUE THAT IT MAKES FOR A NICE ENDING TO A BOOK.

BUT THAT WOULD MEAN CONCEALING THE FACT THAT, IN "REAL LIFE," HIS STORY DIDN'T END WHEN HE GOT TO AIX-EN-PROVENCE.

ONCE THE JOY OF REUNIFICATION HAD PASSED, HAKIM AND HIS FAMILY HAD TO FACE THE HARSH REALITY OF INTEGRATION INTO THEIR NEW COUNTRY.

FOR THOSE FIRST FEW DAYS, THEY MOVED INTO THE FAMILY APARTMENT.

ACCOMMODATIONS WHERE A PORTION OF THE RENT WAS HANDLED BY A REFUGEE AID ASSOCIATION.

UNFORTUNATELY, AFTER 3 DAYS, THE ASSOCIATION TOLD THEM THEY COULD NO LONGER STAY THERE.
AND THEY WERE FORCED TO LEAVE THE APARTMENT IMMEDIATELY.

FROM THE STREET, THEY IMMEDIATELY CALLED THE RED CROSS, WHO SENT THEM AN AMBULANCE.

SPEAKING ABOUT THIS, HAKIM TOLD ME:

"THE PASSERS-BY WATCHED US. I FELT ASHAMED, EMBARRASSED, HELPLESS."

"IN THE COURSE OF MY JOURNEY, I'D BEEN THROUGH TERRIBLE THINGS. BUT I THINK THAT MOMENT WAS WHEN I FELT IT MOST KEENLY."

"I WAS MADE FULLY AWARE OF MY DROP IN SOCIAL STATUS."

THE AMBULANCE TOOK THE LITTLE FAMILY TO A HOTEL IN MARSEILLE.
HOTEL

"NOT EXACTLY A 5-STAR PLACE," AS HAKIM TOLD ME WITH A LAUGH.

IT WASN'T AN IDEAL PLACE TO RAISE A CHILD, BUT AT LEAST THEY WEREN'T OUT ON THE STREET.

HAKIM KNEW THIS VERY WELL AND RECOGNIZED, EVEN IN THEIR SITUATION, HOW LUCKY THEY WERE.

STARTING THE NEXT DAY, HE BEGAN THE INITIAL STEPS TOWARD GAINING REFUGEE STATUS.

THE PROCESS PROVED LONG AND COMPLEX.

THIS PERIOD IN MARSEILLES WAS VERY HARD ON HAKIM AND HIS FAMILY.
THE ONLY INCOME THEY HAD AVAILABLE WAS THE €20 PER WEEK THAT NAJMEH'S PARENTS WERE LENDING THEM.

HAKIM TOLD ME THEY SKIPPED A LOT OF MEALS DURING THIS TIME.
GRRRGL
GRRRGL

AND THEIR DAYS WERE SPENT WAITING.

WITHOUT A PERMANENT ADDRESS, HAKIM HAD TO SPEND HOURS EACH DAY IN LINE, WAITING TO CHECK IF HE'D RECEIVED AN APPOINTMENT FROM THE PREFECTURE.
THIS WAS THE CRITICAL STEP AT THE BEGINNING OF THE ASYLUM APPLICATION PROCESS.

AFTER TWO LONG MONTHS, THEY RECEIVED NOTICE OF THE LONG-AWAITED APPOINTMENT AND THINGS COULD MOVE FORWARD.

TO START, WHILE THE APPLICATION WAS BEING PROCESSED, THE FAMILY COULD RECEIVE AN ALLOWANCE AS ASYLUM SEEKERS.
CHOMP!
CHOMP!
IT WASN'T THE HEIGHT OF LUXURY, BUT IT MEANT THEY COULD EAT THEIR FILL AGAIN.

AND THEN THEY STARTED LOOKING FOR A NEW PLACE TO STAY, AS LIVING CONDITIONS AT THE HOTEL WERE VERY DIFFICULT.
BOOM! BOOM!
WOULD YOU SHUT UP??

WITH THE HELP OF A REFUGEE AID ASSOCIATION, THEY FOUND A ROOM IN A WOMAN'S HOUSE.
DING
DONG
THERE ARE, IN FACT, PEOPLE WHO VOLUNTEER TO TAKE IN REFUGEES.

HAKIM AND HIS FAMILY WERE BOTH HAPPY AND NERVOUS: THEY WOULD BE LIVING WITH SOMEONE THEY DIDN'T KNOW.
AND THEY KNEW NOTHING ABOUT EUROPEANS' WAY OF LIFE.

ALTHOUGH THE EARLY DAYS REQUIRED A BIT OF ADAPTING, THEY QUICKLY BECAME FRIENDS WITH CATHERINE.

THIS PERIOD WAS VERY REWARDING FOR THEM.
AND FOR CATHERINE, AS WELL. TO THIS DAY, THEY REMAIN IN CONTACT AND CATHERINE TAKES HADI TO THE ZOO.

*TO LIMIT THE BURDEN ON THE HOST FAMILIES.

AND IT WAS DURING THIS TIME THAT HAKIM AND HADI WERE GRANTED REFUGEE STATUS.

IT WAS LIKE THE SKY WAS STARTING TO CLEAR, EVEN THOUGH THEY STILL HAD A LOT TO DO.

THEY WERE ABLE TO START STUDYING FRENCH.

AND HADI WAS ABLE TO START SCHOOL IN LATE 2016.

MOMMY!
DADDY!

HAKIM WAS FINALLY ABLE TO START GETTING ON WITH HIS LIFE, WITH HIS FAMILY.
ITA

fabien Toulmé 2019

FIN

EPILOGUE

A few weeks after our last interview, in February 2018, Hakim and his family were given a place in low-cost housing. This marked their crossing into one of the final stages of their odyssey.

However, they still have a ways to go. Learning French is arguably the most significant challenge. The language is the key to employment and integration . . .

Today, Hakim understands it quite well and speaks it capably. But despite the classes he's taken since his arrival, he doesn't speak it well enough to get a stable job at a company.

As he puts it: "When you've been through what I have, it's not like you're a 'typical' student. In order to learn, you have to feel well, and it took me a long time to really put myself back together after my journey."

A bit like he did during his journey, trying to stay ready for anything, Hakim decided to do what he could while waiting for something better to come along.

He's become a self-employed entrepreneur and divides his time between providing gardening services to individuals and going to markets to sell Syrian culinary specialties that he makes with Najmeh. They're not living in poverty, but by the end of the month things can get tough, which they illustrate with a laugh: "We know the prices of various items down to the penny—that says it all."

By the time we finished our interviews, the hardest thing for Hakim to deal with was not so much his drop in social status (which he had gotten used to) as it was his loneliness.
Today, two years later, he has managed to integrate a little further and has made a few French friends, though not enough. He's resigned to it and tells himself that, in any case, it will never be like it was in Syria. Here, again, he puts things in perspective: "Ultimately, the important thing is that we're safe."

If Hakim had to make this journey again, he'd do it without hesitation. Especially when he thinks of his children and their future.
And what about Hadi? You may be wondering how he's doing. How did he recover from his grand journey across Europe?

As of this writing, Hadi is six years old, and Hakim doesn't think he remembers their odyssey.
Or at least, he hasn't spoken to Hakim about it yet.
Hakim has decided to bring it up with him next year.
I should note that the journey has left its traces on him, psychologically speaking.

In Turkey, Hadi often went to the beach with his parents, and he loved it.
Since reaching France, he's been very afraid of water.
Following counseling with a therapist, he's started to open up, but for a very long time he didn't communicate with adults or with the children at school.

Today, he is in first grade, he has friends in his class, and everything is going well. "Hadi even gets invited to birthday parties," Hakim told me happily. "He's thrilled!"

Hakim has built a very strong relationship with his son: "Sometimes when I see him playing, I feel a wave of joy and sadness come over me—it's very strange."
"I hug him and tell him how much I love him and how happy I am to be here with him."

Hakim's second son, Sébastien (born in France during the time of our interviews), is now three years old and has started kindergarten.
"He's very good in class," Hakim told me proudly. "Like Hadi!" he added. "My sons are great students!"

I speak of Sébastien as his second son because the year 2020 saw the arrival of a third: Anwar. "Najmeh would love to have another, to try for a daughter, but I'm not sure I want more kids. And what if we have another boy, haha!"

Although integration is relatively difficult for Hakim, he feels that his children are becoming more French than Syrian.
"Hadi's always saying 'merci/de rien' . . . for everything!"
"Just this morning, I gave him some cake, he said 'merci' and then he scolded me because I didn't say 'de rien' back, haha! Which is very French!"

Hakim hopes that, despite everything, when it comes to their relationships with family and friends, his children will stay in touch with their Syrian side.

Among all of Hakim's siblings, two are now abroad (one brother is in Germany and another in Austria) and five have remained in Syria with his mother. They still live in his old neighborhood, which is almost completely destroyed and where the elderly, women, and children now make up 90% of the population.

They are safe for now, as the fighting has moved to other parts of Syria. But life is difficult there, because everything is very expensive; Hakim tries to help by sending them money when he can.

One of his sisters gave birth to a disabled child. He's paralyzed.
The doctors say it's because of the chemical weapons the regime used while his sister was pregnant.

Do you remember Jawad, Hakim's brother who disappeared after one of the protests (see Book 1)? Hakim told me that he was recently released after seven years in prison, during which time everyone thought he was dead.
"I talked to him recently on the phone. He's changed a lot because what he went through was very hard. He's afraid of everything. He's seeing a therapist to try to get better."

Hakim has also received updates from some of the people he met throughout his journey:

His cousin Mahmud, with whom he started his nursery, moved to Austria. He got married and had kids. He's doing well there and has even managed to start a new nursery.

Ghazi, the friend who hosted Hakim in Beirut, ended up leaving Lebanon. It was becoming difficult for Syrian nationals to live there, given the risk of arrest by Hezbollah. Today he lives in Norway. He's married to a Syrian woman and has a son.

Zahed, his friend from Antalya, ended up going back to Syria. He never managed to raise the money he needed to start the business he dreamed of, and he couldn't make enough to survive in Turkey. Today he lives in central Damascus, a relatively safe part of Syria.

His aunt and uncle who hosted him in Amman are still there.
They continue to live off odd jobs and are hoping that their lot will improve.

His cousin Omar, the Michael Jackson fan, seems to have finally figured out how to talk to girls, because he has a kid now!

As for the pharmacist Nihad and his family, who accompanied Hakim for a large portion of his journey, they are now in Germany, in Dortmund.
They've been granted refugee status and hope to resume their lives in this new country.

You may also be wondering what Hakim thinks of *Hakim's Odyssey*!
"It's good! It's good!" he told me in a very artificial tone.
Sensing my disappointment at his somewhat half-hearted response, he explained: "I tried to read it, but it's a little tricky with my level of French, haha! Anyway, a lot of my friends have bought it and they tell me it's great."
"And Najmeh and I also monitor comments online to see what people are saying about it.*"
"In any case, it's a great way to show people who we refugees really are."

Finally, I asked Hakim how he saw his future.

I'll leave him with the last word: "I miss my family and friends very much. My nursery too . . . I put so much energy into it, but hey, it's probably been destroyed by now, like a lot of things in Syria.
But at this point the idea of returning to live there seems impossible to me.
As long as Bashar al-Assad is in power, it's too risky for me.
So we're going to stay in France.
We've started putting down new roots here: it would be hard for the kids to go back to a country they don't know.
France has really made us feel welcome. The vast majority of the French are very nice, very friendly.
We've gotten a lot of support.
And I haven't really had bad experiences because of my background or my refugee status.
At some point I'd like to start a new nursery here and do the work that I love.
But there's still a long way to go to get there, because it takes a lot of money.
And before that I have to improve my French.
But the most important thing is that Hadi, Sébastien, and Anwar are happy and well, whether that's here or in Syria.
Because everything I did, I did for my children.
I'm so happy when I hear Hadi talking to me about school, and his friends . . .
Remember when we first met, I said I was telling you my story for Hadi, so he'll know where we come from, what we went through.
Eventually, when my children are old enough to understand, I will have them read your book.
And I hope they will be proud of us, and where they come from."

Bordeaux, January 2020

*So I would kindly ask that you leave only glowing comments, thank you (editor's note).

UNHCR

The United Nations Refugee Agency (UNHCR)* believes that the refugee issue must be treated as a global concern, and Hakim's story reminds us that our attention must be focused on the things that really matter: dignity, rights, and humanity.

Many thanks to Hakim and his family for sharing their story of hardships and dangers, to Fabien Toulmé for putting all his talent into listening to this family, and to Delcourt for publishing this moving and hopeful story.

Let us never forget those who have lost their lives in exile, in the Mediterranean and elsewhere, and all those who have had to leave everything behind in order to survive and who now triumph, every day, in the face of adversity.

This essential account ties in with the ongoing commitment of UNHCR and its partners to provide help and lasting solutions to the most vulnerable.

The sheer number of people who have been forced to relocate is one of the greatest challenges of our time. We can face it, but only if we act together.

Vincent Cochetel, UNHCR Special Envoy for the Central Mediterranean Situation

*More information at https://www.unhcr.org

To the migrants who disappeared before they could find their refuge.

Thanks to my editor, Yannick Lejeune, for his help and advice; thanks to Patricia Haessig-Crevel and Laura Crevel-Floyd for connecting me with Hakim and for their help when the project ran into issues; thanks to interpreters Manuel, Bouchra Petit, and Michel Nieto for their indispensable aid; thanks to Leslie Perreaut and Alberto Campi for the photo documentation; thanks to the teams at Delcourt who helped this book see the light of day; thanks to you, reader, for following this odyssey since the first book; and my heartfelt thanks to Hakim, Najmeh, Hadi, and Sébastien for their patience and generosity.

Library of Congress Cataloging-in-Publication Data

Names: Toulmé, Fabien, 1980– author. | Chute, Hannah, 1992– translator.
Title: Hakim's odyssey / Fabien Toulmé ; translated by Hannah Chute.
Other titles: Odyssée d'Hakim. English
Description: University Park, Pennsylvania : Graphic Mundi, [2022]– | "Originally published as L'Odyssée d'Hakim, volume 3 by Fabien Toulmé, Editions Delcourt, 2020."—Book 1. | Contents: Book 3. From Macedonia to France.
Summary: "An account, in graphic novel format, of a young Syrian refugee and how war forced him to leave everything behind, including his family, his friends, his home, and his business. This narrative follows his travels from Macedonia to France"—Provided by publisher.
Identifiers: LCCN 2021017308 | ISBN 9781637790311 (hardback)
Subjects: LCSH: Refugees—Syria—Comic books, strips, etc. | Forced migration—Syria—Comic books, strips, etc. | Syria—History—Civil War, 2011—-Refugees—Comic books, strips, etc. | LCGFT: Graphic novels.
Classification: LCC PN6747.T68 03913 2021 | DDC 741.5/944—dc23
LC record available at https://lccn.loc.gov/2021017308

Printed in Lithuania by BALTO Print
Published by The Pennsylvania State University Press, University Park, PA 16802–1003

Graphic Mundi is an imprint of The Pennsylvania State University Press.

Translated by Hannah Chute
Additional lettering and art reconstruction by Zen

Originally published as L'Odyssée d'Hakim, volume 3, by Fabien Toulmé

The Pennsylvania State University Press is a member of the Association of University Presses.

It is the policy of The Pennsylvania State University Press to use acid-free paper. Publications on uncoated stock satisfy the minimum requirements of American National Standard for Information Sciences—Permanence of Paper for Printed Library Material, ansi z39.48–1992.